T0323980

Cambridge Elements ≡

Elements in Earth System Governance
edited by
Frank Biermann
Utrecht University
Aarti Gupta
Wageningen University
Michael Mason
London School of Economics and Political Science

SUSTAINING DEVELOPMENT IN SMALL ISLANDS

Climate Change, Geopolitical Security, and the Permissive Liberal Order

Matthew Louis Bishop
The University of Sheffield

Rachid Bouhia
UNCTAD

Salā George Carter
Australian National University

Jack Corbett
Monash University

Courtney Lindsay
ODI

Michelle Scobie
University of the West Indies

Emily Wilkinson
ODI

CAMBRIDGE
UNIVERSITY PRESS

Shaftesbury Road, Cambridge CB2 8EA, United Kingdom

One Liberty Plaza, 20th Floor, New York, NY 10006, USA

477 Williamstown Road, Port Melbourne, VIC 3207, Australia

314–321, 3rd Floor, Plot 3, Splendor Forum, Jasola District Centre, New Delhi – 110025, India

103 Penang Road, #05–06/07, Visioncrest Commercial, Singapore 238467

Cambridge University Press is part of Cambridge University Press & Assessment, a department of the University of Cambridge.

We share the University's mission to contribute to society through the pursuit of education, learning and research at the highest international levels of excellence.

www.cambridge.org
Information on this title: www.cambridge.org/9781009565332

DOI: 10.1017/9781009389174

First published 2024

A catalogue record for this publication is available from the British Library

ISBN 978-1-009-56533-2 Hardback
ISBN 978-1-009-38916-7 Paperback
ISSN 2631-7818 (online)
ISSN 2631-780X (print)

Sustaining Development in Small Islands

Climate Change, Geopolitical Security, and the Permissive Liberal Order

Elements in Earth System Governance

DOI: 10.1017/9781009389174
First published online: December 2024

Matthew Louis Bishop
The University of Sheffield

Rachid Bouhia
UNCTAD

Salā George Carter
Australian National University

Jack Corbett
Monash University

Courtney Lindsay
ODI

Michelle Scobie
University of the West Indies

Emily Wilkinson
ODI

Author for correspondence: Jack Corbett, jack.corbett@monash.edu

Abstract: The viability of small island developing states (SIDS) is threatened by three distinct processes – a backlash against globalisation; rising geopolitical competition between great powers; and accelerating climate change – which are pulling at the threads binding the liberal international order together. This Element suggests that this order has been kinder to SIDS than is often acknowledged because its underpinning norms – sovereign equality, non-interference, and the right to development – are inherently permissive and thus provide SIDS with choices rather than imperatives. Their leaders should fight for the continuation and enhancement of that order rather than be seduced by alternatives. The authors provide a rationale for and examples of policies to achieve this, including reforms to the way ODA is measured, debt restructured, climate finance allocated, and global governance organised. These enhancements represent a plausible pathway for SIDS in a period of global upheaval. This title is also available as Open Access on Cambridge Core.

Keywords: SIDS, Pacific, Caribbean, Indian Ocean, climate change, Geopolitics, Development, liberal order

ISBNs: 9781009565332 (HB), 9781009389167 (PB), 9781009389174 (OC)
ISSNs: 2631-7818 (online), 2631-780X (print)

Contents

Preface

Prior to the Glasgow COP26 in 2021, we were asked by the UK's Foreign Commonwealth and Development Office (FCDO) to produce a short podcast to sensitise some of their staff to the problems faced by Small Island Developing States (SIDS). Like many attempts by academics to engage with policymakers, we never discovered whether anybody listened to that podcast or found it useful. But the effort of putting it together – while we were all trapped in our home offices during the pandemic-induced lockdowns – initiated a collaborative process that has snowballed inexorably and catalysed an agenda about which we all remain hugely passionate. In 2022, this was formally institutionalised as the Resilient and Sustainable Islands Initiative (RESI) based at ODI in London. RESI aims to act as a scientific advisory network for SIDS and their development partners. This Element represents a synthesis of what the seven RESI Co-Directors think about islands and their future, with a particular eye on the Fourth UN International Conference on SIDS ('SIDS4') that took place in May 2024 and the Antigua and Barbuda Agenda for SIDS (ABAS) that emerged from it.

Our argument is that SIDS have arrived at a 'critical juncture' at which their viability is threatened by three distinct processes – a backlash against (neoliberal) globalisation; rising geopolitical competition between great powers; and rapidly accelerating climate change – which are pulling at the tenuous threads that bind the liberal international order together. We suggest that this order, although far from perfect, has been somewhat kinder to SIDS than is often acknowledged because its key underpinning norms – sovereign equality, non-interference and the right to development – are inherently permissive and thus provide them with 'choices rather than imperatives' (Sharman 2017: 560). The existence of such choices has been central to their sustainable development. We think SIDS leaders should fight for the continuation and enhancement of that order rather than be seduced by alternatives, such as a return to a self-help system or the institutionalisation of an even more muscular liberalism. We provide examples of policies that would achieve this, including reforms to the way Official Development Assistance (ODA) is measured, debt restructured, climate finance allocated, and global governance organised. Pursuing these enhancements, while perhaps too modest for some, represents the most plausible pathway forward in a period of significant global upheaval.

RESI is a distinctly contemporaneous creation, spanning as it does multiple institutions, countries, regions, and time zones. It is rendered possible by the collaborative technologies of our age: Zoom, Teams, WhatsApp, and Google Drive. This Element is imbued with all the strengths and weaknesses of these ways of working, including the ability to synthesise a breadth of material by writing simultaneously and asynchronously as a team, while unavoidably trading off some depth and a singular authorial voice. This Element has been written on planes and trains as well as in hotels, airports, cafes, and even, sometimes, perhaps rather archaically, in rooms where some of us are sat together, somewhere in the world, with others dialling in virtually on a laptop screen, and of course our respective homes (but rarely our institutional offices). Indeed, the rhythm of post-COVID academic life is such that barely a word was written while physically present on a university campus.

We wanted it to be an Element because the longer form remains the best way to communicate enduring ideas that influence the world for the better. But, compared to the tomes of old, this one is bound by a strict word count and more likely to be read online than in print. The content also reflects the form and the purpose of RESI: we wanted to engage an audience wider than our academic colleagues. So, the arguments are, at times, polemical, and there are no footnotes. You will have to take us at our word (and our other writings) that we have read considerably more than we have cited. Yet we remain heavily indebted to the academic communities that formed us, particularly those who have retained a stubborn commitment to studying and supporting the *small* when the countervailing pressures pull in the opposite direction towards the *big*. There are far too many of you who have influenced us over the years to write every name down. You know who you are. If you do not, a quick glance at the editorial board of *Small States and Territories* journal is not a bad place to start, nor are the reference lists of our other papers, the acknowledgements in our earlier books, and, indeed, the ever-growing list of RESI Affiliates – comprising dozens of like-minded experts from around the globe who share our passion for SIDS and constitute our global advisory network – on our website: https://odi.org/en/about/our-work/resilient-islands/.

We do need to single out a few people for their special influence on both this work and the development of RESI, during what has been the most exciting and rewarding period of our careers. Martin Garrett at FCDO commissioned the original podcast and inadvertently set a ball rolling which is still gathering pace. Alan Whaites, previously the head of the FCDO SIDS Unit, saw a gap in the market for a think tank, and suggested we try to fill it. We hope we have gone some way to repaying the faith he showed in us, without which we might not have had the confidence to apply for the funding under the UK's Small Island Developing States Capacity and Resilience (SIDAR) Programme that has sustained RESI on the first stage of its journey and made this Element possible. Others in the policy world have supported our work and shaped our thinking: Rebecca Fabrizi, the UK Special Envoy on SIDS, and her colleagues Kiran Atwal, Ciara Coughlan, Olivia Goldin, Melanie Moffat and David Finan of the FCDO SIDS Unit; Simona Marinescu, Sai Navoti, Tishka Francis and Miniva Chibuye, vocal champions of SIDS within the UN system; Margot St John-Sebastian and Sharon Lindo of AOSIS; and numerous small state diplomats, especially Ambassador Fatumanava-o-Upolu III Dr Pa'olelei Luteru of Samoa, Ambassador Walton Webson of Antigua and Barbuda, and Tumasie Blair, Deputy UN Permanent Representative of Antigua and Barbuda. Tom Long and Niheer Dasandi, from Warwick and Birmingham Universities respectively, generously provided incisive comments on our initial proposal that significantly sharpened our thinking and pushed us to clarify crucial elements of the argument. Frank Biermann saw value in the idea, the peer reviewers he selected helped us tighten the final draft, and the team at CUP expertly assisted us to finalise the manuscript. As usual, any errors, in fact or interpretation, are our own.

1 Sustaining Development in Small Islands

This Element makes the case for a fresh outlook on the unique development challenges of SIDS. It is published at what is a 'conjuncturally sensitive moment' (Marshall 1998) in which the global order is shifting. Such moments do not present themselves very often, but, when they do, they represent genuine forks in the road. The Fourth International Conference on Small Island Developing States – 'SIDS4' as it is known colloquially – held in Antigua and Barbuda in mid-2024 sought to resolve the distinctive development challenges of this subset of countries (see Lindsay et al. 2023; Bishop et al. 2023). The programme of action it catalysed – the Antigua and Barbuda Agenda for SIDS (ABAS) – will have to become a genuine departure from the status quo if these unique territories' 'special case for sustainable development', as mandated and reiterated by successive UN programmes of action, is to be given meaningful effect.

The choice we face, as a global community, is whether to continue to pursue the norms that are central to the post-war order – that is, the right to development, sovereign equality and non-interference – in which SIDS had considerably greater autonomy than is conventionally recognised, or abandon it and try something else. We look back to assess the patterns of struggle that have characterised development in SIDS from the postcolonial era to the present, before sketching out the varying implications of how different scenarios might produce different outcomes. We conclude that SIDS should fight for the enhancement of the permissive liberal order as the future most likely to produce the 'least bad' development outcomes, both for them and the wider world.

A Fork in the Road

The 1990s was, until now, the most significant – and certainly the most auspicious – decade for SIDS in the postcolonial period because the critical mass they attained in the international system – comprising a fifth of UN members – helped to instigate a degree of collective cross-regional island consciousness. This was, in turn, reinforced by an unambiguous sense that SIDS faced a range of analogous, pressing challenges (Corbett et al. 2021). The SIDS agenda thus arose in an era in which these island states were either taking their first tentative steps as young nations or recovering from the traumatic commodity crashes of the preceding decade and confidence in post-colonial ideas about the merits of national developmentalism had been shaken (see Payne and Sutton 2007). But in retrospect, many SIDS benefitted from the 'permissiveness' of this period – albeit unevenly, and with significant distributional inequalities – as they worked hard to transition away from preference-based agriculture to exploit new niches in emergent services sectors (more on this in Section 2). By dispensing with state-led developmentalism, they also became more assertive about the way their small size created unique economic and environmental vulnerabilities.

In 1990, prior to the second World Climate Conference, thirty-nine countries established the Alliance of Small Island States (AOSIS), which helped create the SIDS label, and then spent the next few years disseminating it assertively throughout the UN system as part of the early round of global climate change negotiations (Ashe et al. 1999; Sutton 2001; Betzold 2010; Corbett et al. 2019). Working through AOSIS, they ensured the 'special case' of SIDS was captured in Agenda 21 of the 1992 United Nations Conference on Environment and Development (Ashe et al. 1999). Recognition of the special vulnerabilities of small island communities was not new, but it was given moral impetus by impending climate change (Corbett et al. 2019). By the mid-2010s many international organisations (IOs) had recognised the SIDS agenda and had dedicated hubs and workstreams, a remarkable achievement given that mainstream theories of International Relations (IR) would predict that these are the countries 'least likely' to influence global affairs (see Keohane 1969).

But since this relative high point, the world has become considerably harsher for SIDS. The three norms that led to an unprecedented era of 'permissiveness' noted earlier all came under severe strain by the end of the 2000s. Geopolitically, the unipolar moment was remarkably short-lived: the hubris of the post-9/11 Iraq invasion in 2003 demonstrated not the extent of American power, but its limits, and it revealed fissures in multilateral institutions that have only spread further, infecting every IO to some degree. Economically, the overconfident certainties of the 'Great Moderation' were rapidly called into question as neoliberal globalisation hit the rocks during the Global Financial Crisis (GFC) of 2008/9 (see Helleiner 2010). Environmentally, as the frequent alarms sounded by climate scientists coincided with ever-more harrowing real-world disasters, it became clear that what we now call global warming is accelerating and likely to exceed numerous planetary tipping points sooner than expected (Wunderling et al. 2021). These processes are, to a significant degree, the result of changes in the global balance of power, in which the relative economic decline of the West was mirrored by the concomitant rise of 'the rest' or the so-called 'BRICS' countries, and especially China (Bishop and Murray-Evans 2020).

For SIDS, this means that the rules shaping their interaction with IOs have not kept pace with the reality of their developmental predicament: depending on the territory in question, this is generally a mixture of volatile growth, elevated debt burdens (usually in the Caribbean) or aid dependence (often in the Pacific), severe exposure to external shocks, and therefore drastically accentuated vulnerability. Conceptually, opponents of differentiation have questioned whether the concept of vulnerability is a useful way of distributing development assistance and concessional finance (for discussion see Corbett 2021, Chapter Five). By contrast, small state experts have increasingly questioned whether a narrow measure of GNI per capita remains an adequate measure of development in SIDS (Robinson and Dornan 2017; Bishop et al. 2023). Practically, IOs have questioned whether SIDS can absorb assistance and generate the types of gains that ODA and concessional finance generate elsewhere. SIDS have responded by attempting to develop better measures of their unique conditions, including the recent UN Multidimensional Vulnerability Index (MVI). This attempts to show in a 'data-driven manner' the intersecting ways in which SIDS are vulnerable and, on this basis, justify their case for 'special and differential treatment' (SDT). But the technical solution is yet to shift the political landscape.

This resistance matters because it is occurring at the same time as the conditions that have underpinned economic development in SIDS are rapidly deteriorating and critical funds are not forthcoming (Wilkinson et al. 2023). In general, ODA to developing countries has declined, albeit with a marginal increase in 2020, largely through donations of COVID-19 vaccines (Prizzon 2022). But SIDS have suffered significant losses over the past decade (Wilkinson et al. 2023). This mirrors the broader decay in the liberal multilateral order that has characterised the post-global financial crisis period. As implied earlier, departing metropolitan powers expected SIDS to continue to rely on agriculture – generally bananas, sugar, and copra – as the basis of their postcolonial development model (Bishop 2013). In contrast to contemporary opinion that the lack of agriculture in SIDS is a result of scarce land and distance to export markets, the shift from the GATT to the WTO in the mid-1990s was a catalyst for the removal of EU concessions, which in turn led to the collapse of agricultural export commodities by the turn of the millennium (Payne 2006; Heron 2011). This was replaced by tourism and financial services, both of which had enjoyed a global boom from the 1980s (Connell 2013). This new economic model brought levels of development in many SIDS that were the envy of many other larger postcolonial states. But they were vulnerable, too: 9/11 led to increased regulation of financial services and, over time, ever-greater forms of oversight and monitoring (Vlcek 2007). Tourism is prone to global market fluctuations – brought on by events such as the global financial crisis and COVID-19 in which it quite literally ground to a halt – and its long-term success is threatened by climate change. The upshot is that SIDS are in desperate need of SDT at the very moment at which their agenda is stalling in IOs.

The geopolitical context, as evidenced by the Trump presidency, China's rise and its relationship with its periphery, including Hong Kong, and the fact that armed conflict has returned to continental Europe, is also changing. The direction of travel appears to be the potential unravelling of the post–Cold War liberal order (e.g. Nye 2017; Ikenberry 2020). This may present some opportunities but also an increased existential threat to SIDS as the structurally weakest members of the international system. Amidst this flux, we ask: what does genuinely sustained development mean for SIDS?

Our Argument: Enhancing the Permissive Liberal Order

Academics and policymakers have spent much of the late twentieth and early twenty-first centuries framing the development challenges faced by SIDS as the dynamic consequence of inherent vulnerabilities and forms of resilience (see, for example, Baldacchino and Bertram 2009; Briguglio et al. 2009; Mycoo 2018; Kelman 2020; Moncada et al. 2021 for discussion). Vulnerability was said to arise directly from small size and isolation which produced diseconomies of scale that dramatically magnified the impacts of exogenous shocks (e.g. extreme weather events, global economic downturns, or pandemics). Resilience arose from the inherent advantages of small size, including the ability of SIDS to engage in niche forms of 'enclave capitalism' (e.g. financial services, tourism, and sovereignty sales). For some, those emphasising vulnerability were too deterministic because of the focus on what SIDS cannot do rather than what they can. This trapped them discursively, limiting the constraints facing them to endogenous weaknesses rather than systemic inequalities

(Lee and Smith 2010). For others, those emphasising resilience could be excessively voluntaristic and over-optimistic about the extent to which the agency of SIDS can transcend their inherent vulnerability: no matter how developed a small state becomes, it will always be highly exposed to sudden and disproportionate shocks that can reverse that development to a relative extent that simply is not the case for larger countries (Bishop 2012).

This framing allowed academics and policymakers to explain the unique condition of the group but also variation between individual SIDS whose distinct trajectories are said to be a consequence of shifting vulnerability, on the one hand, or resilience, on the other. We do not seek to relitigate these debates here. In our view, it is unarguable that the extent of SIDS resilience is unavoidably embedded within the contours of their inherent vulnerability, and this does, in turn, derive from their size, remoteness and insularity (Bishop et al. 2021a). They are, therefore, not two sides of the same coin, but rather alloys from which the coin is mixed, intrinsically and inseparably integrated with each other (see Hay 2002). Our specific intervention in this Element turns on the crucial, but unacknowledged, point that the vulnerability-resilience framing focuses primarily on intervening variables – that is, shocks and capacity – rather than the underlying norms of the international order on which they depend and are notably *permissive* (Sharman 2015, 2017). The permissive order is contingent on the establishment of the UN in 1945 and subsequent decolonisation. But its current form was codified by the adoption of the UN's Declaration of the Right to Development in 1986. The evolving shape of this order remains vital to comprehend what sustainable development means for SIDS because permissiveness is the essence of their 'special case'. SIDS have the biggest stake in the maintenance of key twentieth-century norms – sovereign equality, non-interference, and the right to development– because they underscore their differentiation and thus survival. By starting our account with permissiveness and survival we provide a clearer articulation of what development means for 'special case' countries, and how it might be created and pursued beyond more resilience and less vulnerability (Bishop et al. 2021a).

By 'permissive' we mean a liberal order that upholds the three norms mentioned earlier: sovereign equality and non-interference, which are enshrined in the UN Charter, and the right to development (see Sharman 2015, 2017: 560–61 for discussion). In a permissive liberal international order, the norms of sovereign equality and non-interference are upheld regardless of the size and ability of individual states to defend themselves against armed conflict. The consequence is that a state as small as Tuvalu (population, 11,000), that does not maintain a standing army but has the same vote in the UNGA as China (population,

1.4 billion), faces limited systemic pressures to seek military protection from larger states. Likewise, in a permissive liberal international order the imperatives of the economic self-help principle are somewhat reduced by the provision of foreign aid, with many Pacific SIDS recipients of the highest levels of ODA per capita in the world (Dornan and Pryke 2017). To be sure, some Pacific SIDS also remain designated as Least Developed Countries (LDC) by the international community, which raises questions about how useful ODA is for achieving development in SIDS, and sea-level rise presents an existential threat to low-lying atoll states, rendering questions about economic viability in relation to size irrelevant. Nonetheless, the acceptance of these norms ensures that:

> Instead of imperatives, the international system provides microstates with a menu of options from which they craft different strategies. These states have taken a pick-and-choose approach to their sovereign prerogatives: energetically wielding some, delegating others in selectively forming hier-archical relationships, and commercialising still others. The variation whereby some micro-states delegate or sell sovereign prerogatives while others do not demonstrates that these strategies are indeed choices, rather than products of systemic necessity. (Sharman 2017: 560)

Indeed, Sharman notes that small states have delegated fewer sovereign preroga-tives than much larger and wealthier members of the EU (Sharman 2017: 561). The upshot is that, rather than competitive selection, in which economic viability or security predetermines the survival of states under anarchy, under a permissive liberal international order, small states not only survive, but they exercise auton-omy. And if that order is enhanced, this self-determination might continue to sustain their development.

Intellectually, this is a similar argument to that outlined by the critical IR scholar Amitav Acharya (2014, 2018), who has emphasised that world order is not something that rests solely on the material power of hegemons: it is *constructed* (and contested) on the basis of shared (or resisted) norms and practices. Three specific ideas from his work chime with our analysis here. One is that these norms are also *reproduced by* non-hegemonic actors who *reshape* them; they are not passive recipients *of* them. Another is that existing order is breaking down in the wake of decaying US hegemony, leading to what Acharya calls a 'multiplex world' with 'both risks and opportunities for managing international stability' (Acharya 2017). This means that elements of 'order' and 'disorder' can exist simultaneously. A third is the notion that globalisation will not disappear: it will change in form and become less western-centric as the 'rising powers' accrue ever-greater economic power (see Bishop 2016). Where we differ (slightly) from Acharya is the implication that we are only now entering the post-American world. Mainstream IR has spent much of the post-2008 period worrying about this question; however, many working in critical International Political Economy (IPE) actually date the end of US hegemony to the economic crises of the late 1970s, and the emergence of contemporary *neoliberal* globalisation (see Bishop and Murray-Evans 2020). The crucial point is that this marked the moment at which the United States (US) was no longer truly 'preponderant' across all domains of hegemonic power, and could not decisively recast world order in its own image (Payne 2005).

Perhaps ironically, it was also a period – in retrospect – during which many SIDS navigated a range of destabilising economic upheavals to exploit the 'globalisation niches' that emerged to great effect. The issue, from their perspective, is less that world order destabilised, and more that a period in which permissiveness was at its height may now, since the twin 2008 and 2020 crises, be giving way to something considerably less so. We are, of course, not trying to suggest that everything was rosy under neoliberal globalisation. While the causes of the climate crisis can be traced back to European industrialisation, it has accelerated rapidly under this order, which has so far also proven incapable of reversing course. A permissive order has also reproduced, in many ways, neocolonial relationships and patterns of control that are undoubtedly inequitable. This is in part because the liberalism on which that order was based was often honoured in the breach, masking the enduring pursuit of self-interest on the part of powerful states, along with the bending of IOs to serve their interests, or disregarding them when this was resisted (Muzaka and Bishop 2015). Moreover, for SIDS specifically, this epoch brought with it a range of thorny problems that we discuss in the Element, including the defeat of national development projects, the imposition of structural adjustment, reduced trade policy space, painful economic transformations, elevated debt burdens, the rise of illicit economies and violence, and accentuated demographic and social inequality. Neoliberal capitalism was, then, far from perfect. Indeed, a more 'embedded liberal' form of globalisation – reflective of the kinds of social democratic compromises that existed between 1945 and the late 1970s – would likely have been *more* permissive (see Bishop and Payne 2021a). This is the future order we argue SIDS should seek to create.

In making this case we must first admit, to our surprise, the hitherto unacknowledged benefits *of* a permissive liberal international order. In retrospect, it was, to some degree, 'better' than many possible alternatives that may have existed. The US hegemony on which it was anchored certainly constrained the options of many SIDS, perhaps most infamously in the brutal destruction of radical political experiments in places like Grenada and Jamaica in the 1970s and 1980s or the advancement of American corporate interests in the 'banana trade war' that decimated export agriculture in other Eastern Caribbean islands in the two decades that followed (Clegg 2002). But it also provided – certainly in theory, if not always in practice – the public good of international order and relatively open markets on which their successful adjustment depended. In this sense, it offered opportunities that, crucially, might not have existed in a *less* permissive order, something that appears increasingly evident today as US hegemony is an advanced state of decay (Cooley and Nexon 2020) and the neoliberalism of the recent past has given way to much darker forms of more monopolistic and exploitative 'disaster', 'surveillance' or 'cannibal' capitalism (Klein 2008; Fraser 2022). These morbid tendencies have only intensified through and beyond the COVID-19 pandemic, essentially extending and worsening the stagnation that came in the wake of the global financial crisis (Tooze 2021; Baccaro et al. 2022). The relative permissiveness that existed prior to this witnessed the promotion of IOs and myriad global governance regimes in which SIDS could participate and pursue their interests – even leading initiatives as norm entrepreneurs (Corbett et al. 2019) – and, until now, was undergirded by a comparatively benign natural environment (or, more pessimistically, reservoirs of ecological capital that could be depleted).

Whether or not we agree that the permissive order was mostly good or mostly bad, the key point is that SIDS' ability to exploit it was contingent on a geopolitical context in which interstate conflict was rare, borders were porous, and openness and interconnectedness were prized. These conditions, which the countries we now call SIDS and their intellectuals helped to create during the decolonisation period (Getachew 2019), provided them with a space to identify and exploit niches in creative and innovative ways that leveraged, rather than overcame, the advantages of their small size and peripheral position in global affairs (Baldacchino 2010). If any or all of these conditions, and the institutions that sustain them, are removed, then development progress in SIDS becomes unsustainable (in the economic sense). Rising geopolitical tensions between great powers and climate change are thus potentially existential threats for their postcolonial development model.

What Next for the Liberal International Order?

The term 'critical juncture' is used by political scientists to refer to particular moments in which agents' choices are especially significant (Capoccia and Keleman 2007). These moments are usually only apparent in hindsight – revealed by the backward glance of the historian. But, as mentioned earlier, we know they are important because SIDS have faced such moments before. Our intervention is made in that light. The argument presented in this Element is necessarily tentative, as claims that SIDS face a critical juncture at which they might become unviable have been made repeatedly since the end of the Second

World War (see e.g. Doumenge 1989; Cole 1993). In each instance the alarmism has proven to be false. But rapid change has also occurred, as we saw in the 1990s. Creativity, both individually and collectively, was crucial to this adaptation and we continue to place great stock in the ability of SIDS to shape these changes to suit their developmental needs.

This Element is designed to assist in that effort by mapping out the potential scenarios and consider how SIDS might maintain, and even enhance, the permissiveness of the liberal international order. Our analysis is structured around three potential scenarios: (1) that the order becomes more anarchic, competitive and self-help; (2) that the order moves to a more muscular liberalism; or (3) that the order is augmented to become more permissive. We assess that the third scenario is the most desirable for SIDS and outline the types of strategies and issues that they, and other states who seek to uphold a permissive liberal international order, might champion. Indeed, we go so far as to argue that we can assess how permissive the liberal international order is by the way it treats SIDS as its structurally weakest members. In making this case we borrow heavily from IR theory in particular, with classical realists having long viewed conflict between self-interested states as the inexorable outcome of power imbalances in an anarchic international system. This view is countered by liberals who argue that cooperation can produce order and mitigate anarchy. Each position, at the extreme, reflects the two outlier scenarios – self-help vs muscular liberalism – that we discuss throughout the Element.

These three scenarios are primarily a heuristic or analytic device. We employ heuristics because it helps to think through the issues and possibilities. But they unequivocally should not be confused with facts or be used as a basis for prediction: they are 'rules of thumb' or mental 'shortcuts'. The standard we set for them is that the reader can imagine them occurring. That is, they are plausible possibilities grounded in real-world questions and challenges rather than thought experiments of the type employed by philosophers to establish principles. It is therefore important to state from the outset that each is fundamentally a *tendency of* the *same* order. Aspects of all three have always been latent in the 'real-world' post-1945 order – whether its embedded liberal, neoliberal, or, now, perhaps, 'post-neoliberal' variant – and they will likely exist simultaneously in the future (alongside patterns of order and disorder as suggested earlier). But, the point is that the extent of each, or its effects in specific global policy domains, will differ, and potentially come into conflict with the others. We could certainly imagine a world in which 'muscular liberalism' dominates environmental and economic domains but a 'self-help' scenario pervades security discourse, for example, and the transitions between them may not be as clear and obvious as our stylised account suggests. Yet the most beneficial tendency is, in our view – and on the basis of the analysis at hand – the permissive, and a world in which that orientation is most pronounced vis-à-vis more competitive or muscularly liberal logics is one that is likely to redound to the benefit of SIDS specifically, and larger states, too.

As outlined in our discussion of Acharya, a key building block of our argument is the idea that international orders or regimes, including the climate regime, are social institutions (Young 1998) constituted by norms or appropriate standards of behaviour that reflect what actors consider to be morally and ethically correct (Finnemore and Sikkink 1998). Norms are created by the common understandings of actors based on shared learning, maintained by their inherent legitimacy and reinforced by their incorporation into regulatory and legal systems. These frameworks and structures are characterised by a complexity of actors, institutional interplay, institutional complexes (Gehring and Oberthur 2008), modalities of hierarchy, space, scale and networks that are involved in agenda setting, decision-making, policy implementation, monitoring, and review (Biermann and Pattberg 2008; Dellas et al. 2011). The contestation of key norms is what makes this a critical juncture for SIDS in which alternative scenarios appear possible.

Scenario One: A Less Liberal and More Competitive, Self-Help Order

In the first scenario, the facade of 'organised hypocrisy' (Krasner 1999) of the liberal international order is unmasked, exposing the underlying anarchy of the international system, as evidenced by the return of great power rivalry between China (and perhaps with it, Russia) and the US and its allies. In this version of the future, China's rise in particular, and its limited respect for liberal norms, will force the US to abandon the pretence that it should be bound by multilateral rules, too, as was the case during the Trump presidency (Nelson 2019). This is a contentious argument: Chinese illiberalism has also coexisted until now with a relatively strong, if sometimes partial, defence of global multilateralism, especially in the trade arena (see Bishop and Zhang 2020; Weinhardt and ten Brink 2020), while arguably American commitment to a liberal order has only ever been partial (Hopewell 2020, 2021). Put differently, powerful states embody contradictory tendencies, including that they are supportive of multilateralism as long it also serves their interests. But putting the caveats to one side, the key shift in this scenario is the erosion of all three norms that we see as crucial to a permissive liberal international order: sovereign equality, non-interference, and the right to development.

Initially SIDS may benefit from this system as they play large states off against each other in return for increased financial support and preferential access to specific markets, as is currently occurring in the Pacific (Cavanough 2024). In the long run, however, they face increased security threats as pawns in great power strategies (e.g. Petersen 1998; Corbett 2023), which will plausibly undermine the norm of sovereign equality, in particular. This is the lesson of the Age of Empire and the Second World War and, as realists and neorealists have long argued, this inability to survive under anarchy – or, at best, seek shelter from nearby great powers (Thorhallsson 2018b) – remains an ever-present structural condition for all SIDS (see Pederson 2023). The upshot is that this scenario is likely the worst case for SIDS, and we argue policymakers should be focusing all of their energy on avoiding it despite the short-term benefits it might offer.

Scenario Two: A More Muscular Liberalism and Multilateral Reinvigoration

In the second scenario, the failure of great power expansion – as in Russia's invasion of Ukraine, perhaps – combined with the anti-democratic threat posed by unchecked corporate power, will lead to (neo-)liberal principles being reasserted globally, but in a more muscular fashion. In this view, the key future threat is not interstate conflict between great powers but intensifying collective action problems that require reinvigorated multilateral institutions and 'steering' bodies to solve (Bishop and Payne 2021b). These include the rise of digital platforms, artificial intelligence and the monopolistic transnational corporations they have spawned (Zhuboff 2019); organised crime, money laundering, trafficking in guns, humans, and drugs (Cockayne 2016); increases in non-communicable and vector-borne diseases; plastic pollution; and climate change. States will need to collectively solve these problems by creating new international rules to govern both the metaverse and the Anthropocene, building new institutions for enforcement and distribution of gains. Key to this happening, though, would be some kind of hegemonic accommodation between the US and China to recast global governance and its underpinning norms.

The barriers to this scenario coming to fruition are certainly high, but we are more concerned with the potential implications they posit than the likelihood of the threat manifesting. Initially, this scenario would help SIDS due to the emphasis on participation and inclusivity in a reinvigorated multilateralism. It is not difficult to see potential positives: 'cosmopolitan' liberals have long articulated a vision of how state power – in which excessive inequalities produce conflict and reinforce collective action problems – is subordinated to global institutions and agendas that benefit humankind equally (see Held 2010).

So, a more muscular liberalism would allow SIDS to continue advocating for the bridging of the digital divide, technology and knowledge transfer (particularly green energy), transport infrastructure, improvements in ICT, human resource development and retention alongside institutional capacity development at the state level for better service provisions. It does not, however, guarantee that these requests will be granted. This is especially so in the context of multilateral treaties and rules such as intellectual property rights and local content requirement laws that favour developed countries over developing ones.

Furthermore, in the long run, this scenario will see the norms of sovereign equality and non-interference come into tension with the right to development, because solving global problems will require a degree of uniformity and regulation that will likely come at the expense of differentiation between states. There may also be calls for reciprocity among states, which will further weaken the call for a 'special case' for SIDS. This would create difficulties for all states, but particularly acute ones for SIDS as they have carved out economic opportunities *by* exploiting niches, such as financial services, and *by* enacting diverse forms of sovereignty, such as the sale of shipping registries, passports, and internet domain names. These strategies will become even more difficult to leverage than at present because their exceptionalism will become a threat to the international community as a whole. The upshot is that a more muscular liberalism is not necessarily better for SIDS than the return of great power rivalry.

Scenario Three: A More Permissive Order

The third scenario is one in which permissiveness – defined, previously, by the balancing of the three norms that are central to the current liberal order – is retained and enhanced as the core guiding principle of global governance. This is the scenario we think SIDS should be seeking to achieve because it enables them to participate in multilateral institutions as independent actors imbued with a degree of sovereign autonomy. The point then is that a permissive order is more heavily regulated than a self-help system but that regulation is designed to protect and promote diversity rather than large state interests dressed up as universal goods.

We acknowledge that a permissive liberal international order has not resulted in all SIDS graduating to high income status – although many have – any more than it has negated problems such as diseconomies of scale, narrow sector specialisation, or limited bureaucratic capacity. Moreover, we recognise that some of the strategies that SIDS have adopted are both born of a degree of desperation and contain within them potentially damaging implications for global public goods like tax justice or financial probity. But this is true of all states, many of whose strategies, such as industrialisation or other forms of severe resource exploitation, carry negative externalities which are drastically to the detriment of SIDS, and would likely continue to be so under either of the other two scenarios (as the niches presently enjoyed by SIDS disappeared). To echo Sharman previously, a permissive order has at least ensured they are confronted with a world of choices – albeit often constrained ones – rather than imperatives forced upon them, whether by great powers acting without regard to shared norms and international rules, or, indeed, overweening global bodies acting without regard to (small) state sovereignty. This is the world we think SIDS leaders should attempt to maintain and enhance.

Maintaining Diversity in the Coming Order

SIDS helped create the current permissive liberal international order (Getachew 2019), and this Element starts from the assumption that they can be key players in the formation of the coming order, too. Our claim is that the revival of a permissive liberal international order will require a simultaneous strengthening and weakening of norms and practices of global governance. SIDS need stronger multilateralism because their survival as states depends on the continuance of global norms. They also need multilateral processes to work better, especially in climate finance. But it also must be weakened in relation to forms of conditionality and large state regulation if SIDS are to maintain, let alone extend, the developmental gains made during the late twentieth and early twenty-first centuries. Our hope is that by recasting the debate about their development to focus more on the international governance context that sustains SIDS, rather than the domestic factors that act as intervening variables, we can help to shift international opinion towards more viable alternatives and the kind of 'global bargain' that is required (Bishop et al. 2023).

The types of changes that reformers should immediately pursue include:

1. altering the way development assistance is allocated, as current formulations do not account for relatively wealthy yet highly vulnerable states;
2. generating new forms of debt relief that will arrest the current debt trap in SIDS, releasing funds that can be used to provide better public services and address social issues;
3. improving climate financing mechanisms, so that promised adaptation funds in particular are both easier to access and can be more easily absorbed to strengthen resilience of SIDS;
4. using international law to press for clarity on responsibilities and seek compensation for climate and environmental harms suffered by SIDS;

5. reforming the international financial institutions themselves, particularly the Multilateral Development Banks (MDBs), and ensuring SIDS' priorities are better represented in these changes.

This list is certainly not exhaustive, and these changes may not be transformative in the manner imagined by architects of the New International Economic Order (NEIO) half a century ago (Getachew 2019). But the combination might provide SIDS with a better chance of securing a prosperous future than the rapidly deteriorating status quo. They are a first step. Medium-term options include:

1. expanding but democratising and constraining multilateral organisations. SIDS need representation in the G20, for example, with Singapore a possible candidate and site of a permanent secretariat (see Bishop and Payne 2021b);
2. further reform of the development architecture to recognise the unique circumstances of SIDS and the accumulated historical debts of colonisers; and
3. recasting how IOs support climate adaptation, to include but also go beyond loss and damage compensation, while also recommitting the world to more aggressive targets.

Again, these are illustrative options with the common aim of enhancing permissiveness. The thread that ties them together is that academics and policymakers need to focus specifically on how SIDS' development is enabled and constrained by the global governance architecture and its 'ruling ideas' (Ban 2016). By implication, if the development of SIDS is going to be rendered genuinely sustainable, then global institutions need to become even more sensitive to their distinctive needs (Scobie 2019a). If they do not, an already troubling developmental panorama could see their progress wound back significantly.

2 Small Island Economies

The SIDS economic story is one of marked historical diversity, followed by policy convergence from the latter part of the twentieth century onwards. The former reflects distinct colonial experiences: islands were colonised by different powers, at disparate points between the fifteenth and twentieth centuries, oriented towards discrete extractive practices, with varying levels of intensity. They also exhibited diversity in terms of how far the pre-colonial governing order was subordinated: in some cases it was entirely eradicated, in others it was forcibly accommodated to imperial power, but with variation in the degree of metropolitan oversight. The latter reflects enduring realities of small size in a neoliberal global economy: as the strategies that shepherded many island states to independence after the 1960s – that is, doubling down on often colonially constituted commodity exports, while attempting some degree of industrialisation – fell prey to declining terms of trade and preference erosion, there were few options that SIDS could adopt other than the relentless pursuit of enclave capitalism (Grydehøj and Kelman 2016). This convergence around a set of similar economic strategies to address common challenges – narrow sector specialisation, a heavy reliance on imports, and high levels of exposure to economic shocks – led to the creation of the 'SIDS' label itself to draw attention to the unique condition of small islands (UN 1994). The attendant vulnerability-resilience framing has become the orthodoxy for thinking about island economies (Bishop 2012). But it struggles to explain the shifts that created it, why the critical juncture faced by SIDS today has arisen, and what to do in response. This section offers answers to these questions.

SIDS Economic Development in Historical Context

Caribbean states were among the first to be colonised by Europeans during the so-called Age of Discovery. They imported with them a model of plantation slavery that had first been trialled in the Macaronesian Atlantic islands – Madeira, the Canaries, and the Azores – that remain territories of Spain and Portugal (Greenfield 1977; Fradera and Schmidt-Nowara 2013). Plantation slavery and colonialism continued through the Age of Empire until 1804 when Haiti forcibly seized independence from France (James 2001 [1938]). During this period, these islands were sources of hitherto unimaginable wealth for Europeans, who went to the new world in search of gold and instead found a much more valuable commodity in sugar (Williams 1980 [1944]). Indeed, it is difficult to overstate the wealth – and the immiseration – generated by sugar. In 1763, to settle the Seven Years War, France ceded its continental North American possessions – the whole of Canada and the American mainland east of the Mississippi – for just the island of Guadeloupe, which was considerably less productive than St Domingue [Haiti] or Jamaica. The wealth generated by the transatlantic plantation model, in which slaves were brought from Africa to work Caribbean plantations producing sugar for metropolitan consumption, began to decline from the late eighteenth century, partly due to South American competition and partly due to the emergence of sugar beet production in Europe (Richardson 2009a; 2009b; 2015). Declining profitability was thus a key factor in the decision by metropolitan governments to support abolition, which came into effect for the British Caribbean colonies after Westminster passed legislation in 1833 (Lewis 2004).

A plantation economy was imported to the Indian Ocean and some Pacific islands – notably Mauritius and Fiji – during the nineteenth century (discussed in the next section). The historical parallels end there, however. Despite Spanish explorers venturing into the Pacific during the sixteenth century searching for a different passage to India and later using some islands, such as Guam, as waystations for galleons en route to the Philippines, most Pacific islands were among the last to be colonised. Fiji aside, which still has a sugar industry, the main agricultural crop Europeans sought to cultivate was copra, refined from coconut. This industry was never as lucrative as sugar, and the costs of transport from the region were high, so Pacific island colonies were largely neglected. Colonial administration and associated infrastructure development barely extended beyond capital cities (Firth 1997). Basic education and healthcare were delivered by mission organisations, or not at all. This form of colonisation stands in direct contrast to the intense centuries-long occupation of the Caribbean in which indigenous communities were replaced by wholly new and modern societies created 'de novo' as 'a tabula rasa on which the European colonisers . . . put their imprint as they wished' (Lewis 2004: 3–4).

During the early twentieth century, most of the small islands we now call SIDS struggled to return a profit and thus came to be seen as a burden on metropolitan treasuries. Poverty and underdevelopment were rife, especially in urban settings and among waged islanders. Beyond the reach of the metropole, and especially in the far-flung archipelagos of the Pacific, patterns of pre-colonial 'subsistence affluence' continued (Fisk 1970). In much of the Caribbean, sugar production stumbled on. But it was also marked by a striking sense of decline and decay: labour experienced 'serflike conditions' that were little better than those of a century earlier when slavery ended (Brereton 1981: 85). Indeed, in 1872, British Prime Minister Benjamin Disraeli had already captured the sense of stagnation by describing territories that once generated unimaginable imperial riches as 'wretched colonies', 'millstones round our necks' and 'colonial deadweights'.

This pessimism framed debates about the viability of decolonisation. The Dominican Republic followed Haiti in gaining its independence from Spain in 1865, with Cuba also becoming independent after the war between Spain and the US of 1892, remaining under US rule for four years until 1902. But, elsewhere, SIDS had to wait for the 'winds of change' for the topic of independence to be taken seriously, and even then there was often little enthusiasm for it on the grounds that even if the metropole was able to jettison islands that were otherwise a financial 'burden', their subsequent economic performance – determined as it was by (dis) economies of scale – was unlikely to be a glowing 'advertisement for past rule' (Corbett 2023: 38). Although not always rendered fully explicit, this concern with economic viability unquestionably permeated the politics of decolonisation in small islands. At its most basic, it explains why different groups of states were seen by metropolitan elites to be 'ready' for decolonisation at different times. So, after the largest countries seized independence, it was generally only the next-largest ones that were granted independence in the 1960s and early 1970s, with the smallest territories coming later or even, to this day, remaining non-sovereign.

This led to a debate, which persists today, about how SIDS economies might be rendered viable in practice. The first set of arguments proposed scaling up SIDS economies via regional integration. Put most forcefully in relation to the Anglophone Caribbean by Nobel Prize–winning St Lucian economist Arthur Lewis, the argument was essentially that regional integration would create economies of scale and enable import substitution. When coupled with the pursuit of external capital to kick-start industrial expansion – disparagingly termed 'industrialisation by invitation' by critics – Lewis argued that this model would gradually internalise the growth dynamic and generate a level of development that had eluded the region post-emancipation (Lewis 1954). For a time, he appeared to be correct, with Jamaica and Trinidad, in particular, achieving substantial economic growth in the 1950s and 1960s. But this growth was short-lived. More generally, regional integration collapsed due to the general unwillingness of British colonial officials to provide substantial economic subsidies and as a result the West Indies Federation (1958–1962) unravelled because the larger islands did not want to be locked into an arrangement in which they were perpetually subsidising their smaller neighbours (see Mordecai 1968; Bishop and Payne 2010).

Decolonisation in other islands and regions, which largely occurred from the 1970s onwards, adopted a more conventional nation-state model than the short-lived attempt to create a single, federal, multi-island Caribbean state. It also gave rise to alternative explanations for, and conceptualisations of, economic development in small islands. One of these was dependency theory, an offshoot of Latin American structuralist thought made most famous by Raúl Prebisch and Hans Singer (see Margulis 2017). This encompassed two broad variants: a reformist-structural one associated with thinkers such as Fernando Henrique Cardoso, Enzo Faletto, and Theotonio Dos Santos, and a more explicitly radical Marxian historical-materialist one associated with André Gunder Frank, Paul Baran and Paul Sweezy. Both shared an analysis of the dependency and underdevelopment that afflicted post-colonial societies, but they diverged on the solution: the former viewed 'dependent development' as plausible within wider relations of dependency (Cardoso and Faletto 1979), but the latter argued a more deterministic line of which the only logical conclusion was a rupture with international capitalism (Frank 1967). These debates were mirrored closely by thinkers in SIDS. In the Caribbean, for example, the New World Group (NWG) of scholars at the University of the West Indies (UWI) – comprising many of Arthur Lewis's critics – developed their own distinctive brand of *dependencia*, although many distanced themselves from that specific label (see Bishop and Thompson 2020).

The third theory emphasised the impact of smallness on economic development (e.g. Demas 1965). The 1938 Moyne Report into Caribbean development saw industrial development as largely unsuited to the region, thus resigning it to a marginal future of plantation agriculture and small-scale manufacturing. Fast-forward to the early 1990s and the creation of the SIDS category, we find the prevalence of similar ideas that emphasise how small geographic size means that SIDS lack adequate, exploitable economic resources, resulting in a limited pool of competitive growth sources, which, in turn, fosters undiversified economies. Due to their remoteness and insularity, SIDS face huge challenges in shipping and other kinds of connectivity. They thus suffer from low production volumes and high labour costs, and are unable to compete on the basis of price on their export products. They are also unable to compete on the basis of quantity due to shortage of land and fragile ecosystems, as well as expensive energy supplies (Dornan and Shah 2016). Archipelagic SIDS suffer from additional issues such as inadequate levels of government services, which in some cases harbour resentments (Baldacchino 2020) and thus threaten political unity. Because they are small, these countries are also extremely trade-dependent, importing even basic items as food and fuel, and with a narrow export base, they are extremely vulnerable to external economic shocks (see Heron 2008).

What none of these prior assessments of SIDS economic fortunes predicted is the emergence of 'enclave capitalism' or 'globalisation niches' and, perhaps more importantly, SIDS' ability to exploit them (see Baldacchino 2010; Connell 2013; Rezvani 2014). This was reflected in the boom in the global tourism industry and parallel ability of the smallest states, in particular, to lease and sell sovereignty in the form of financial services and citizenship by investment schemes. Selling globalised services is dependent on a permissive liberal order, which was, as discussed earlier, effectively created by the political structures of the immediate post-war period – including the norms of sovereign equality, non-interference and the right to development – that intensified once the Soviet Union collapsed in 1989, ending the era of bipolarity in international relations. In particular, a world in which violent inter-state conflict was rare (Sharman 2017), reduced the cost of travel and fast-tracked the creation of offshore financial services centres. This led to a shift in development and growth trajectories unimaginable in previous decades (see Buzdugan and Payne 2016).

We can see the impact of these trends when we compare those islands that have been able to participate in forms of enclave capitalism and those that have struggled to do so. Caribbean and Indian Ocean countries are almost all middle- to upper-middle income countries, for example. Likewise, the best-performing Pacific states, such as Palau, Fiji, Vanuatu, and Cook Islands, all have substantial tourism economies (Wolf et al. 2022). The LDCs, by contrast, continue to rely on agriculture and other primary sectors rather than services. The exceptions to this trend are the small number of SIDS with substantial natural resources, such as Trinidad and Tobago, São Tomé and Príncipe, Nauru (historically), and Guyana (in the future).

This correlation is obviously a fairly crude and limited measure of development, and there are many other explanations – size, scale, distance from markets, regional specificities – for why SIDS perform differently in terms of growth patterns. Moreover, high levels of per capita income may not represent intrinsically desirable forms of development, as it could well be maldistributed and come at the cost of severe ecological or social dislocation. Indeed, it is often said that the poorest and least developed of the small Eastern Caribbean countries, Dominica, which has no 'mass' tourism and a tiny airport that does not serve metropolitan destinations, is the happiest and healthiest, with much of its electricity produced by renewables and both the highest life expectancy at birth in the Caribbean and the largest number of centenarians per capita on earth (Government of Dominica 2022). Nonetheless, the point remains that the more that SIDS were able to exploit globalisation niches – whether in tourism or in other services sectors – the more their per capita income seemed to rise. So, the trade-off of a strong environment and social cohesion in Dominica has been limited economic diversification: the inverse to some neighbouring islands which have experienced higher, but more volatile, growth alongside overdevelopment and greater social inequality (see Payne 2008).

In sum, the consequence of these trends is that from the 1980s onwards we could begin to talk about SIDS sharing an economic model distinct from that of other developing countries. To be sure, larger states also have substantial tourism and financial services sectors. But SIDS are almost entirely reliant on them for local income generation because they comprise a disproportionate share of the economy. The model is not without problems, however, as we discuss at length in the rest of the Element. But it is unclear that radical alternatives will offer better outcomes. Rather, we posit that SIDS are likely to achieve more sustained development if we retain and enhance the norms that drove this relative success.

Economic Development and the Future

SIDS have benefitted from a permissive liberal order. But, as outlined earlier, they now face a critical juncture. By considering three alternative scenarios of a changing global order, we throw into sharp relief how high the stakes are for them.

Scenario One: A Less Liberal and More Competitive, Self-Help System

The most obvious alternative to the current order is a return to the self-help system of the Age of Empire in which the larger conquered the smaller. If this occurred, it is unlikely we would see a return to plantation agriculture. Instead, and in the absence of a technological shift in which the ocean, in particular, became a sought-after resource, perhaps for deep sea mining or geothermal energy, a return to unrestrained great power competition would likely see SIDS territories exploited either for geopolitical purposes or by multinational corporations based in powerful countries. This would plausibly lead to a race to the bottom whereby island countries compete to offer ever-greater offers of assistance, tax breaks, and weakening of environmental or social legislation, reinforcing the tendency for value extraction and leakage from the enclaved local economy with few backward or forward linkages.

Geopolitical exploitation has long been the case in the North Pacific, where the US retains its control over Guam, one of the most important strategic positions in its defensive perimeter against China and the rest of the Mariana Islands. It is also intensifying its military presence in the three freely associated states – Palau, Federated States of Micronesia (FSM), and Marshall Islands – via the establishment of a third Compact of Free Association. China's response has been to seek security agreements with other SIDS in the South Pacific. The economic consequences of this are often to the short-term benefit of SIDS who can donor shop and exercise other forms of leverage. The consequence is that for the time being the return of great power competition appears to be advantaging Pacific SIDS.

One potential downside for SIDS in general, which the US and its allies have been at pains to point out, is that Chinese investment is often not as advantageous in the long run as it seems (Wallis et al. 2023b). This rhetoric is difficult to assess (see Zhang and Shivakumar 2017 for discussion), and development assistance and finance from the US and its allies has usually come with substantial conditionalities, too. But the observation does hint at the larger problem for SIDS that the return of a self-help system would entail. Specifically, such a system has little interest in upholding the key norms of a permissive liberal order: sovereign equality, non-interference, and the right to development. The long-running implications of this are likely to be to SIDS' detriment because the erosion of key norms would reduce the ability of states to engage in collective action.

A further weakening of multilateralism and an increase in inter-state conflict would substantially impact on SIDS economies, in part because any increase in cost and risk entailed in international travel would likely reduce the profitability of the tourism sector in particular. We have seen a version of this over the last decade in which revenues from tourism and other sources have been decreasing while the fixed costs of imported fuels, food, and other necessities have been on the rise, especially in recent years due to disruptions caused by the COVID-19 pandemic and the outbreak of war in Ukraine (and then Israel-Gaza). The prices of cereals surged as a consequence of Russia's invasion, for example, causing significant concern for both LDCs and SIDS. This price surge is particularly worrisome for Indian Ocean and African SIDS, like Cabo Verde, Maldives, Mauritius, Seychelles, and São Tomé and Príncipe, where net imports of cereals constitute more than one-third of their total dietary needs, ranking them among the most dependent nations. Negotiations surrounding access to food and fertilisers, which are also crucial strategic imports for the region, quickly became integral aspects in the diplomatic and strategic efforts of both belligerent parties to garner support from nations in the southern hemisphere. The point is that these types of goods are crucial for the economies of most SIDS and their dependence on external partners for imports is much greater than that of other middle-income developing countries.

Strategic imports could also be weaponised. At the macroeconomic level, this would imperil the balance sheets of SIDS governments and increase their dependence on aid and loans. SIDS private sectors would continue to lag behind and be unable to foster structural transformation, as (large, multinational) firms in FDI-source countries would strengthen their monopoly positions as a way of shielding their assets against rivals, with few benefits for (small, domestic) SIDS businesses. In a context of frictions, foreign investors would be also wary about granting loans and purchasing bonds from SIDS, and it would be more challenging to reach sustainable debt restructuring programmes in case of repayment difficulties. Critical readjustments would be necessary, and SIDS would likely be pressured into signing disadvantageous investor-state dispute clauses in bilateral agreements. In a self-help system, such clauses – whereby investors force governments to make changes to policy and legislation that favour private accumulation while shielding them from democratic oversight – could conceivably find their way into many more areas of law beyond simply state-to-state trade agreements. But, because of the relative breakdown of multilateralism, global arbitration will be less stable. This is also a possible scenario, but with different consequences, under a more muscular liberal order (see subsequent discussion).

Those SIDS with large natural resource reserves, including Trinidad, Guyana, Timor-Leste, and, to a lesser extent, Jamaica might be somewhat insulated from these negative economic consequences. In theory, these countries could benefit from increased inter-state competition if it pushed up commodity prices. However, an excessive reliance on commodities in the economies of these SIDS poses the risks of so-called 'Dutch disease', with serious potential consequences for continued economic and social development, as well as governance (John, Papyrakis, and Tasciotti 2020; Hosein 2021). Moreover, in practice, higher commodity prices would also come with heightened risk in a self-help system because they would increase the likelihood of conquest and occupation. The value of those resources is increasingly apparent to malign external actors that covet them: it is, then, unsurprising that, as global attention was focused on Ukraine and Gaza in late 2023, the Venezuelan government chose to intensify its long-running, simmering dispute with Guyana over the oil-rich Essequibo region, raising the prospect of an actual military intervention. These kinds of episodes will only intensify under a self-help era, where small countries have fewer resources – beyond support from other powerful patrons – to resist.

In sum, even during a permissive era where the US is the rhetorical standard-bearer of global liberalism, they regularly exerted power in ways that transgressed liberal norms to the detriment of the smallest states. These tendencies would only intensify under a self-help scenario, which would likely be, on balance, to the economic detriment of SIDS. Some might make short-term gains by donor shopping or from higher commodity prices. But the impact across the group would likely still be negative and, in the long term, many would even struggle to survive as independent states, facing the very real prospect of increased dependency and even recolonisation.

Scenario Two: A More Muscular Liberal Order

Given the potential consequences of the return of a self-help system, it is tempting to assume that SIDS would be better off championing a more muscular liberal order in which regional and global institutions set the agenda and regulate compliance via system-level rules. If the WTO had greater teeth, for example, Antigua and Barbuda might have been compensated after winning its gambling dispute with the US in 2007 (Jackson 2012). Likewise, climate action could be more advanced, with reduced emissions and warming ensuring the survival of low-lying atoll states. Indeed, there are many more environmental examples, which we will cover at length in Section 4. For now, the important point is that, while it appears on the surface that collective action via stronger multilateral institutions would be the best scenario for SIDS, this is not necessarily the case. The reason for this is that these assumptions overlook the fact that the current permissive order, despite being under threat, is made up of competing norms and the tension between them that ensures SIDS are faced with 'choices rather than imperatives' (Sharman 2017: 560). A more muscular liberalism would likely continue to champion the right to development for all peoples, for example. But it would be less concerned with upholding norms such as sovereign equality and non-interference. Indeed, it would invariably come to see these norms as being in conflict: the very notion of *state* sovereignty, which implies diversity of performance and outcomes, would come into conflict with the utilitarian imperative to deliver a model of development that delivered greatest good for the greatest number.

A more muscular liberalism would therefore inevitably reproduce some of the most malign tendencies of the neoliberal era out of a desire to resolve these tensions. The most obvious way this might occur is that those SIDS most reliant on ODA would see the emphasis on partnership and collaboration decline, replaced instead with an intensified language of universal values and standards, along with technical fixes rather than national development plans and programmes. This reliance on conditionality and one-size-fits-all technical fixes is already a problematic feature of 'projectified' development assistance in general (see Hout 2012) and its pervasiveness in the development panoramas of SIDS has been roundly and widely critiqued (Meki and Tarai 2023). We acknowledge that some degree of technocratic governance is evidently necessary for embedding multilateral compromises and maintaining a relatively open, liberal, global economy. But, even before a global financial crisis that fully laid bare the intensification of global inequality that had accelerated under neoliberalism, it was clear that it had – along with widespread, disfiguring financialisation – gone too far, constraining domestic democratic choices without sufficient corresponding democratisation at the global level (see Rodrik 2011).

More problematically, the successes of SIDS over the last three decades rested on globalisation's essential incompleteness and the patchiness of governing regimes, thus enabling them to create enclaves and exploit niches. By contrast, a renewed muscular liberalism would plausibly see this patchiness filled in. The upshot is that, under this type of order, some people from SIDS – particularly those already imbued with high levels of social and finance capital, including dual citizenships – may find greater individual opportunities for exploiting an even-more aggressively liberal rules-based order. But, island societies as a whole would have even less choice than at present over how they are governed, and certainly so in terms of advancing unorthodox state policies. We argue this would likely have negative net consequences for their economies.

Finally, the promise of liberalism is often honoured in the breach and transgressed by powerful actors *anyway*. The most obvious precedent is colonialism, which rested on liberal ideas about progress (Bell 2015) but, in practice, entailed benign neglect at best, and slavery and exploitation, at worst. For this reason, the idea that local communities and their leaders are best placed to make local decisions was the main argument in favour of decolonial self-determination. We acknowledge that some SIDS have subsequently experienced periods of poor local governance, and that even when governed well the types of economic transformation that independence leaders imagined has often been more difficult to realise than anticipated. But it is also important to recognise that their current development model, which involves identifying and exploiting niches, would be unlikely to have arisen but for entrepreneurs capable of exercising choice amidst a permissive order, be they locals or expatriates. For this reason alone, then, a more muscular liberalism should be resisted by SIDS, too.

In sum, a more muscular liberalism would have some benefits for SIDS, especially if it meant IOs could regulate large state excess and non-compliance, divert Northern resources towards Southern development, and facilitate trade and migration 'from below' (Connell and Corbett 2016). But the danger is that it would likely come at the cost of sovereign equality and non-interference, which would be experienced as a loss of control. The entire SIDS agenda of the last three decades can be distilled to the core idea that what works for other countries will not necessarily apply to the condition of small islands, which is unique. The existence of the SIDS grouping thus presumes and champions the virtues of diversity while a more muscular liberalism would necessarily require uniformity in both word and deed. In the extreme, it could lead to a scenario, especially under climate change, where IOs, which favour universalist principles and technical fixes, decide that continued investment in sinking or disaster-prone small island territories is not worth the returns. This would represent the worst existential threat to SIDS.

Scenario Three: An Enhanced Permissive Liberal International Order

The final scenario, and the one we advocate for as the 'least bad' option, is that the permissive order is retained and enhanced. By this we mean that the key norms which readers will be familiar with by now – sovereign equality, non-interference, and the right to development – are held in tension, ensuring that island leaders remain faced with choices rather than imperatives (Sharman 2017: 560). We posit that, all things being equal, SIDS are likely to achieve the best development outcomes when they are able to take as much control over their economic trajectory as possible. That control will be far from absolute, and likely constrained – even the very largest countries do not have the power to bend the global economy to their will – but under an enhanced permissive order there will be more room to manoeuvre than in the other two scenarios. Here, we outline why that will be the case before concluding the section with a discussion of the types of policies SIDS should pursue to enable and then maximise the advantages of such a system.

The main economic advantage of a permissive liberal order is that – in theory, if not always in practice – it guarantees sovereignty regardless of size and the capacity of the state to enforce it. Most SIDS do not have standing armies. Those that do will never be in a position to engage in open conflict with other small islands, let alone great powers. Yet they face a very low likelihood that they will be conquered. The nullification of the basic security imperative of states in a self-help system reduces their costs – armies are expensive to create and maintain – while ensuant peace enables them to engage in forms of multilateral trade and migration that have increased their GDP/GNI per capita. As noted earlier, international tourism depends on a world in which inter-state violence is rare. The ability to claim statehood while never having to enforce it militarily has also enabled SIDS to lease and trade sovereign prerogatives, including via offshore banking, citizenship by investment, flags of convenience, diplomatic recognition, and so on. The upshot is that their niche-based economic models are contingent on the norm of sovereign equality in which they are treated – again, in principle, at least – as full members of the international community regardless of their size (Sharman 2015, 2017). Of course, they face a series of disadvantages in exploiting their autonomy: global governance and the wider global economy are evidently tilted towards serving the interests of the most powerful. But SIDS have also had substantial success in driving forward agendas as norm entrepreneurs and exploiting opportunities *because of* their right to participate in global affairs that arguably belies their diminutive stature (Bishop 2012).

A second reason why a permissive liberal order is advantageous for SIDS economies is that it upholds the norm of non-interference. This is especially important for types of non-tourism economic activity that come under the umbrella of 'sovereignty sales'. Tax havens benefit high net-worth individuals in larger states but not their governments, which lose tax income. They have attempted to crack down on this industry via the global 'blacklisting' regime (Vlcek 2007). But it survives and is increasingly spreading beyond the West to incorporate Eastern, especially Chinese, capital, too (Vlcek 2014). The same principle applies to other sovereignty sales – including citizenship-by-investment and the sale of access to EEZs for fishing – as well as those that might emerge in the future, such as blue bonds. Non-interference also enables SIDS to sell sovereignty bilaterally and even when other countries might oppose the arrangements. As we have seen, the US rents tracts of territory in the North Pacific for military purposes, despite opposition from the USSR in the past (Teiwaki 1987). Australia effectively leases Nauru and Manus Island in Papua New Guinea (PNG) for the purposes of housing asylum seeker detention facilities that have attracted considerable criticism on human rights grounds (Storr 2020). Crucially, though, the ability of SIDS to pursue these sources of income is largely protected regardless of opposition from other, bigger, states.

The final reason why a permissive order is beneficial to SIDS economies is that it upholds the right to development. This norm is especially important for ensuring they have access to ODA and other forms of concessional finance. Many SIDS claim that they are not sufficiently benefitting from this norm, with GNI per capita representing an ossified measure determining entitlement rather than the vulnerability that shapes their unique developmental problématique (Bishop 2012; Bishop et al. 2023). This, in turn, is why they need an MVI to be used by donors to increase volumes of concessional finance available to them (Wilkinson and Panwar 2023). Yet, equally, it does not follow that they do not benefit at all or in the aggregate. Indeed, Pacific SIDS receive among the highest levels of ODA per capita in the world (Dornan and Pryke 2017). Moreover, the fact that the countries we now call SIDS were able to create their label in IOs, and use it to advocate for their 'special case' and mechanisms like an MVI is contingent on the idea that all states should have a chance to improve their economic condition. A self-help system nullifies that right and SIDS would have to compete for it amidst greater anarchy, while a more muscular liberalism would uphold it for individuals (and private firms) but less so states, which raises the possibility of universalist models and even forced displacement under climate change. By contrast, the current order commits to enabling SIDS to pursue their right to development within the boundaries of political units created in the aftermath of the Second World War and regardless of their suitability into the future. The order may not have made good on that promise, and it may well be experiencing a degree of decay. But its existence provides grounds on which they can appeal for more advantageous conditions.

Towards a More Permissive Liberal International Order

Economic development remains contingent on a permissive liberal international order that helps provide long-term, reliable, and cheap development finance. How, then, might SIDS work, individually and collectively, to achieve this?

SIDS are already adept at advocating for their unique needs and circumstances to be recognised, and have pushed particularly hard for the MVI to be adopted and used as a complement to GNI per capita, which is a weak measure of material welfare or well-being, particularly for SIDS where it overstates their relative level of development (see Bishop et al. 2021a: 15–16). The MVI offers a common method for identifying and prioritising those countries with severe structural vulnerabilities, and has given SIDS renewed hope and impetus to the 'beyond GNI per capita' agenda. Indeed, it could become, as the UN notes, 'a vital tool to help small island nations gain access to the concessional financing that they need to survive the climate catastrophe, to improve their long-term national planning, service their debts, and sign up to insurance and compensation schemes that may be their last hope when the waters rise' (for a discussion, see Bishop et al. 2023). But it is not clear yet how donors or MDBs will use the rankings and information about vulnerability in their finance allocations. For the MVI to unlock more finance for SIDS, it needs to gain strong buy-in from across international financial institutions.

Bilateral donors allocate ODA according to their own policies and priorities, but, according to rules set by the OECD Development Assistance Committee (DAC), countries with a GNI per capita above USD$12,695 (in 2020) are no longer eligible and graduate from the list. This excludes eight SIDS that are considered high income. MVI scores could be used to inform the graduation process – potentially providing those countries with high levels of vulnerability additional assistance and more time to strengthen resilience before graduating – but all DAC members would need to agree, and there is strong resistance from some quarters. Nonetheless, engagement between DAC members and SIDS is growing thanks to an OECD DAC-AOSIS taskforce, initiated in 2022, and this will help bring the special circumstances of SIDS to the attention of more development partners. In particular, recognition of aid ineffectiveness in SIDS could lead to further guidance being produced for DAC members and emphasis being placed on long-term capacity building, strengthening of data systems, and prioritisation of finance that strengthens resilience in SIDS.

MDBs are another critical component of the multilateral system and major provider of development finance for SIDS. Set up after the Second World War, but before many SIDS existed, for a long time they ignored the special needs of SIDS partly because engaging them was considered too costly and complex: SIDS have far fewer experts staffing the departments that engage externally; their financing needs are generally perceived as too small (yet also too risky) to be worthwhile facilitating; and they are thought to lack capacity to manage large investments (Bishop et al. 2023). The World Bank and Asian Development Bank (ADB) have developed special 'exceptions' categories for SIDS so they are eligible for – and receive determined allocations of – grant finance regardless of income level. But how they do this is very different, and other MDBs do not make any exceptions for SIDS. The result is that overall levels of financing to support resilience in SIDS remain low in relation to levels of vulnerability (Wilkinson et al. 2023). This is a problem, because it intrinsically undermines the sovereign equality and right to development that they are supposed to enjoy.

Problems still abound when it comes to concessionality for SIDS, because ODA (primarily grants and concessional loans) is predicated on being temporary, so recipients are supposed to outgrow their need for it *by developing* and thus graduating from the DAC list. SIDS simultaneously have to convince the international community that such finance can generate developmental progress, while implicitly arguing that, because of their structural vulnerability, they may require development assistance into perpetuity. These tensions are inherent in the contemporary MVI process. On the one hand, SIDS are treading a fine line in arguing they are (uniquely) vulnerable due to their distinctive characteristics, while implicitly leaving open the possibility that other states might be too – the MVI being a universal UN index, which does not necessarily capture the main features of vulnerability in SIDS specifically. On the other hand, they are also implying that the MVI is not solely about accessing greater shares of finance to which many of them are not presently entitled, yet maintain hope that it achieves precisely that once implemented (Bishop et al. 2023: 3).

Use of the MVI alone will not lead to a radical shift in the SIDS condition. But it can help ensure their survival in an economic, environmental, and geopolitical environment that is rapidly changing. Moreover, initiatives like this – which are both multilateral in intent while also potentially finding exceptions and derogations for specific country needs – are only conceivable, even if not always honoured in full, under a permissive, rather than self-help or muscularly liberal, order. Development finance will continue to be needed by SIDS to invest in opportunities and improve their condition, albeit in an incremental way. For some, this will be seen as a disappointing concession to the limitations of global capitalism. We acknowledge this and will explore it more fully in the next section. We also appreciate that development in SIDS has been uneven, with not all countries and regions benefitting equally. Nonetheless, it is important to recognise that the economic model developed by SIDS in the 1980s and 1990s has often been a remarkable success. That success was contingent on specific political and economic circumstances, however, and the lesson for SIDS is that they should seek to maintain and enhance these conditions into the future, while also mitigating their negative effects, which we will discuss further in the next section.

3 Small Island Societies

Globalisation has, in certain respects, been a boon for SIDS, confounding the expectations of many critics. However this growth has been, if not illusory, certainly replete with tensions and paradoxes, especially as it relates to wider patterns of social development. For one thing, many small islands have become over-dependent on one sector, usually tourism, which generates desperately needed foreign exchange, but brings with it an array of negative externalities, imposes social and environmental costs, and often functions as an enclave with weak linkages to the local economy (Bishop 2010). This in turn makes growth exceptionally volatile: when global shocks happen – as they have with the two 'once in a generation' crises just a decade apart in the global financial crisis and COVID-19 pandemic – the industry grinds completely and suddenly to a halt. This can decimate a country's fiscal position instantly, eviscerating employment and undermining the social contract. In fact, services in general, because of their relative labour intensity and volatility, generate more precarious and unpredictable work than did agriculture (Lee, Hampton, and Jeyacheya 2015). The upshot is that, while SIDS have clearly experienced growth, it has not led to the kind of broad-based development that many in their communities desired or hoped for at the dawn of independence. There are multiple interrelated reasons for this.

SIDS Societies in Historical Context

It is hard to overstate the extent to which SIDS are, in general, products of their distinctive historical and geopolitical positioning. As we saw in the previous section, in the Caribbean, pre-colonial society was almost-entirely wiped out by colonisation, with a completely new Creole society transposed onto it. By contrast, European colonisation came relatively late to the Pacific, did not completely eradicate existing society, and its administrative writ did not travel far beyond capitals. This reflected, in part, the archipelagic nature of many Pacific states, their remoteness and insularity, and the relatively limited wealth available to colonisers. By the time colonisation began in earnest in the 1800s, trans-Atlantic slavery was already being abolished and sugar was declining in value. So, with some partial exceptions – indentured labour in Fiji and 'black-birding', meaning coercing or kidnapping indigenous people from Vanuatu or the Solomon Islands to work in servitude in Australian plantations – Pacific colonists could not create analogous plantation societies. Because their economic objectives differed, they often sought to minimise their interference in – and in some cases even protected – traditional ways of life by discouraging white settlers and disallowing land claims (Firth 2000).

Nonetheless, the divergent experiences of colonialism in disparate SIDS regions converge in one place: that is, the generation of enduring legacies and social characteristics (or pathologies) that can be traced back to the earlier colonial experience. These effects are reproduced daily, whether through patterns of ethnic stratification or island secessionist pressures; modes of cultural organisation and interaction; the nature of community and familial organisation; ongoing forms of violence and intergenerational trauma; and even quotidian mores, such as dietary preferences that weigh heavily on contemporary health outcomes (see Wilson 2016, 2023; Thompson 2020). In short, colonialism had – and still has – negative impacts everywhere, whether ensuing state forms are larger or smaller, and regardless of the extent of the horrors experienced in individual societies. These effects are therefore ongoing – albeit uneven in their scope – and substantive decolonisation is not a one-off event, but an ongoing process that continues into perpetuity (Banivanua Mar 2016).

Crucially, its effects are evident in the patterns of inequality and injustice that we see across SIDS. Partly in recognition of this, the early post-colonial period entailed an attempt to right these wrongs by creating more just, fair, and equitable societies. In the Caribbean, this meant the creation of social democracies in which political parties (on both sides) had their roots in a powerful trade union movement whose platforms invariably included strong social rights, institutionalised tripartism, and free healthcare and education. Elsewhere, the absence of plantation agriculture ensured that trade unionism did not take the same form (Bishop, Corbett, and Veenendaal 2020). Consequently, the maintenance of traditional institutions amidst modernity was seen by some as an attempt to ensure forms of social redistribution persisted (White and Lindstrom 1997). In the Indian Ocean, Mauritius – which experienced indentureship like Fiji, Trinidad, and Guyana – combined interventionism with a high level of trade openness and social welfare, generating sustained growth and development alongside a vibrant democracy in an ethnically complex society (Lindsay 2018). By and large, most SIDS did not trial socialism or communism, with the exception of important but short-lived experiments in Grenada, Jamaica, and Guyana, and the somewhat anomalous case of Cuba, which has a significantly larger in population than most SIDS but is usually included in the group.

Over time, these systems of redistribution and reciprocity, whether state-led or traditional, have weakened. There are several explanations for why. The first is that emergent neoliberalism undermined early attempts to recast the post-colonial state as a more just and equitable arbiter of domestic economic relations. This was apparent from the unravelling of the NIEO, of which SIDS were champions, and continued via structural adjustment imposed by the IFIs and MDBs (Buzdugan and Payne 2016). Privatisation, deregulation, and liberalisation were largely imposed from outside and regardless of their suitability: 'discussions about development were no longer ones of grand design developed within the region, for the region, but about how best to administer the programmes that were designed elsewhere under the neo-liberal paradigm' (Sutton 2006: 59). This process proceeded unevenly across SIDS as a whole, depending on their capacity to resist the imperative of liberalisation or exploit it in the pursuit of growth. The paradox of these 'pseudo-development strategies' (Baldacchino 1993) is that they drove growth but also aggravated social inequality.

The second reason for a weakening of social welfare systems in SIDS is that this is simply the nature of capitalism, which depends on and encourages individualism (see Sonenscher 2022). Yet capitalism in general, and neoliberal globalisation in particular, are not impersonal forces that result from divine intervention, but rather irredeemably political processes (Bishop and Payne 2021a). Caribbean countries were certainly constrained in their options, but the wider context was shaped by the preferences of powerful actors, primarily the US and EU (Girvan 2010). We see similar arguments in the Pacific, but in reverse: economists still bemoan the collectivist inclinations of islanders, including gifting surplus capital to relatives and kin rather than using it as the basis for investment, along with the fact they persist with collective land tenure when private property rights would stimulate growth (Duncan 2008). In all cases, the argument is that, while individualism is taking root in Pacific societies, it has not gone far enough to achieve developmental gains. Yet if we prioritise equity rather than growth, then it is arguable that the Pacific's resistance to neoliberal mores is potentially the very thing that has preserved high levels of social capital, and this in itself is evidence *of* development, albeit of a different kind.

A third, related set of arguments is that, rather than mitigating poverty and social exclusion, the interaction between small size and collectivist cultures has led to the domination and exploitation of SIDS by key personalities and their families who have sometimes treated their populations as personal 'fiefdoms' (Crocombe 2008). In the Pacific this is often referred to as neo-traditionalism or patrimonialism (Morgan 2005). But we see similar patterns in other SIDS, too, with certain families often synonymous with the politics of specific islands – for example, the Birds in Antigua (Gascoigne 2023) – despite the absence of so-called 'traditional' cultural practices. An optimistic reading of this would be that dominant leaders simply reflect electoral popularity and governing competence: the Barbados Labour Party under Mia Mottley, for example, won successive elections in 2018 and 2022 with a clean sweep of all thirty seats. And, despite having held office for almost twenty-five years as this Element went to press, Ralph Gonsalves of St Vincent actually sought to decentralise power in an ultimately unsuccessful constitutional reform process in the 2000s (Bishop 2011). Nonetheless, whether the cause is population size, political system, or culture, the argument runs that the anticipated outcome in most SIDS is, at best, clientelism, and, at worst, cronyism, nepotism, and corruption, all of which undermine development (Stone 1986).

A fourth set of arguments are grounded in critiques – often postcolonial and feminist ones – of religion. Specifically, they see religiosity and the dominance of Christianity, in particular, as ensuring that small states remain conservative societies, to the detriment of some sections of the population, including most obviously women and sexual minorities. But this also affects everyone in some way, such as through resistance to sex education in schools or the retention of misogynistic laws and customs. Despite being signatories to the UN Conventions on the Rights of the Child (CRC) and Elimination of All Forms of Discrimination Against Women (CEDAW), adolescent marriages remain prevalent in some Pacific countries, including Solomon Islands, Marshall Islands, Nauru, and PNG (see UNFPA and UNCIFEF 2022). The region also has the lowest levels of women's representation in democratic politics globally (Baker 2018). Numerous states have, or have recently had, just one or two female MPs, or even none at all. For some scholars, this form of patriarchy is a relic of a particular type of imported religion that arrived with colonialism but is alien to indigenous culture. Some Pacific societies are matriarchal, for example, and others retain a distinct third gender with religious conservatism sitting uneasily alongside traditional belief systems (Schmidt 2016). Similar arguments are sometimes made about Creole religions and practices such as Obeah, Vodou, and Rastafarianism in other regions. Either way, the point, to return to where we started this section, is that the social settlement in SIDS is blighted by problematic gender norms and practices, often intersecting with racialised hierarchies, that reflect the colonial inheritance (Barriteau 1998; Barrow 1998; Morgan and Youssef 2006). These can, in turn, lead to yawning labour market inequalities and sizeable gender pay gaps (ILO 2020) and a triple, quadruple, or even quintuple burden, where women are responsible for domestic labour, paid work outside the home, and the mental and emotional labour associated with caring for children and the elderly.

In sum, a permissive liberal order has produced mixed results for social development in SIDS. The positive effects include obtaining noteworthy levels of – albeit exceptionally volatile – growth that has maintained reasonable living standards and good health and educational outcomes relative to international comparators. The downside is persistent poverty, inequality, and social exclusion. Indeed, tourism infrastructures are themselves emblematic. They have generated jobs, but for limited numbers of predominantly younger people, offering low wages, while enjoying enormous tax breaks and other subsidies, with working conditions waxing and waning alongside upheavals in the global economy. The sector has also colonised limited public space, especially beaches, leading to the implicit – even explicit – exclusion of local people, and reshaped local cultures in often-problematic ways, while reproducing familiar side effects, including severe pressure on scarce natural resources, especially water, permanently blighted natural landscapes and the provision of often-illicit tourist services, such as sex work and drugs (see Lee, Hampton, and Jeyacheya 2015). All of this will be exacerbated, in multiple complex ways, by accelerating climate change, the imperatives of a 'just' transition, and wider questions of island ecologies and mobilities, which we discuss in the next section (Bishop et al. 2021b).

Small Island Societies and the Future

The mixed results for SIDS societies produced by the permissive order can explain why many commentators and policymakers would favour the development of a radical alternative. But we think this risks too much, and instead champion the enhancement or augmentation of a permissive liberal order as the best way to manage these pathologies rather than the return of a self-help system or the creation of a more muscular liberalism.

Scenario One: A Less Liberal and More Competitive, Self-Help System

A less liberal and more competitive self-help system of capitalist globalisation would not be tempered by social democratic ideas about self-determination or the right to development, and would therefore likely increase poverty, inequality, and social exclusion in SIDS. Under this scenario, the pathologies we discussed at length in the previous section would likely worsen an already problematic social settlement, which in some SIDS includes high levels of criminal activity and violence. This is a future that the most pessimistic commentators have long predicted (e.g. Cole 1993) but by and large has been avoided in most SIDS most of the time.

The 'doomsday' view would reinforce all forms of social exclusion and poverty, including those related to gender discussed earlier. But perhaps the most historically harrowing for these regions in particular would be the reassertion of racialised hierarchies, which are, of course, already latent in a permissive system that is yet to truly begin transcending them (Sassen 2014). Any order in which a handful of great powers rule and multilateral institutions – especially notions of sovereign equality – decay will, over time, reinforce and reproduce the mores of the most powerful, and that power will likely become imbued with ideas of technological, moral, and potentially racial superiority. These tendencies have always been latent in the ideas underpinning US hegemony – and are particularly evident in both the neoconservatism of the early 2000s and the Trumpism of the 2020s – just as they are in Xi Jinping's Han nationalism. It is not difficult to envisage a highly competitive world where such narratives evolve to justify both new forms of neocolonial control and plunder *and* the weakening of the right to development and multilateral development assistance, to the obvious detriment of SIDS.

Scenario Two: A More Muscular Liberal Order

We might expect a more muscular liberal order that aggressively upholds the right to development to be able to mitigate some of the problems SIDS face. Potential benefits include reinforced multilateral institutions, strong global rules, and meaningful sanctions for transgressing them. There is no doubt that a focus on human rights could advantage certain groups who have been marginalised in SIDS. A more muscular liberalism would also ensure SIDS survive and their needs continue to be taken into account in the systems and processes of global governance. But the same problems identified in the previous section, such as the erosion of the norms of non-interference in particular, would likely result in SIDS being subjected to uniform laws and off-the-shelf technocratic solutions that are, at best, wasteful and, at worst, detrimental to their development.

This might include even worse access to development finance, despite a stronger commitment to development on the part of the global community, because SIDS would be seen as either less deserving than poorer countries or poor investments due to their small populations. A more muscular liberalism would also likely shut down forms of enclave capitalism. We can see the potential for this to occur in debates about a global minimum tax rate, which attempts to solve the problem of tax evasion that is crippling larger states, enabling them to advance redistributive policies, but, in doing so, undermines the viability of SIDS that rely on offshore finance for revenue. This would further impact debt burdens, which would likely increase alongside even more volatile growth due to an over reliance on tourism, further reducing fiscal space. In general, then, because a more muscular liberalism would be less likely to recognise the unique circumstances of any nation, including SIDS, it would ultimately lead to worse social outcomes overall, even if the rights of certain social groups are championed.

Scenario Three: An Enhanced Permissive Liberal International Order

The argument in favour of augmenting the permissive liberal order is that it enables the three principal norms to be balanced against each other. The right to development ensures that SIDS are able to draw on assistance from larger states and multilateral institutions, but at the same time the norms of sovereign equality and non-interference would remain in place ensuring that SIDS have a say in how that assistance is used. We dismiss arguments outlined earlier about these countries not being best placed to address their social problems. Indeed, claims that they experience endogenous problems with local culture fail the most basic empirical tests given the diversity of SIDS with similar development challenges. Likewise, while democratic politics is practised differently in SIDS to elsewhere, it usually involves forms of redistribution and the protection of key social institutions, such as collective land tenure, that mitigates against poverty and social exclusion (Corbett and Veenendaal 2018, Chapter Two). Religious arguments are clearly important explanations of gender-based discrimination, but religious institutions are also key avenues by which social services are delivered in SIDS, especially with weakened state capacity due to neoliberal reforms and a private sector not large enough to provide alternatives in areas such as healthcare and education.

The upshot is that, in our view, the main reason SIDS are seeing increases in poverty, inequality, and social exclusion compared with the early post-independence period is the inability of IOs to fully embrace their special circumstances. This has led to the intensification of neoliberal reforms – a version of a more muscular liberalism – combined with global trade policies that advantage the largest at the expense of the smallest. The solution is that larger states need to recognise that SIDS cannot thrive under a neoliberal system unless it entails carve-outs through SDT that accommodate their unique needs. If they want to persist with these structures and associated protectionism for their own industries, they will need to provide ongoing financial assistance for SIDS and facilitate – rather than shut down – their ability to exploit niches and deliver basic services. Other options include either instituting a global trading regime that better enables SIDS to compete with them or entering nonreciprocal bilateral agreements. The latter is the least ideal of the two, as such arrangements tend to put SIDS in a weaker bargaining position, providing powerful counterparts with the ability to unilaterally withdraw benefits at any time.

Towards a More Permissive Liberal International Order

There is no single policy that will heal the intergenerational impacts of colonisation, global capitalism, patriarchy, and ethnic division on island communities. Some commentators and policymakers will argue that nothing short of radical re-ordering of the type envisaged by the architects of the NIEO will do. Maybe that is true. But as the previous scenarios illustrate, radical alternatives create their own problems, too. Besides, no amount of re-ordering will change the geographical factors that make SIDS vulnerable: that is, small population size, remoteness, and insularity. These factors make them, by their nature, dependent on a permissive external environment. Therefore, rather than starting again, this Element unapologetically argues that we can augment the current order to improve their condition. Put differently: we can build a better globalisation that simultaneously strengthens multilateral governance while expanding the options for SIDS to pursue their developmental ambitions within it.

A critical way of achieving this is, first and foremost, to expand the fiscal space available to SIDS. In one sense, this is an economic, rather than social, solution, but local resource mobilisation is the most straightforward way for the state to deliver social services and enhance wellbeing. Moreover, the two are intimately linked. These services – health, education, social security, and other social (and environmental) intervention programmes, as well as policing – are almost-always the first to be jettisoned when a fiscal crunch happens, and this in turn negatively affects the capacity of a small country to mobilise the finance necessary to invest in resilience. The consequence is that stagnation can occur, in terms of both the capital stock available (including, of course, social capital) and the everyday quality of state services. By the same token, the opposite is true: the more fiscal space SIDS have to invest in those services, sustaining healthy, highly educated and peaceful societies, the more likely they are to then build and maintain high-quality infrastructure and other capital stock, in turn helping to create resilience.

Yet many are struggling with unmanageable and highly volatile debt burdens: numerous SIDS are amongst the most heavily indebted countries globally, some carry debt-to-GDP ratios of well over 100 per cent of GDP, and these can cost as much as 30 per cent of GNI to service or even 50 per cent of government revenue. As we discuss in the next section, these also tend to be the countries that experience frequent external shocks and – because of their relatively high GNI per capita – have the worst access to concessional financing. So, increasing fiscal space, whether through debt relief or other novel mechanisms, is critical to expanding the scope for social investments in SIDS. In many respects, this is the most elegant solution: reducing debt burdens, or mitigating the risks that lead SIDS to build up elevated debt piles, would be the most effective form of development assistance, not least because it would leave them in control of their own social spending.

The international community also has a responsibility to increase fiscal space in SIDS precisely because they suffer disproportionately from a lack of it, and would, if it were expanded, benefit disproportionately too. Moreover, in a world where many of their challenges stem from participation in a deeply unequal international order inherited from colonialism – where huge wealth was extracted from them – which is still structured in many respects according to neocolonial logics, this would also have the effect of representing some degree of reparatory justice (see Beckles 2013). At present, SIDS struggle to deliver quality education, healthcare, water and sanitation, electricity, security, and safety nets to their populations. Bringing debt down to sustainable levels is, at the technical level, undeniably complicated and full of political tension, and it will require different kinds of mechanisms to restructure and reduce current debt burdens, as well as strong public financial management systems and instruments that can help build reserves and smooth public spending in the future. Debt relief should be a greater developmental boon than any other source of financing, but developing tailored policies that can be applied to increase fiscal space in a diversity of individual country situations is tricky, partly because there are significant data gaps. SIDS need support on debt management, and to negotiate with creditors and bring down the cost of borrowing. But the key point, as with ODA, is that SIDS need a new global bargain that reflects their unique condition.

Under a more permissive liberal international order, SIDS can push the international community to develop innovative finance mechanisms to ameliorate the tight fiscal situation in which they are often trapped. SIDS have been first movers in developing green and blue bonds to increase sustainable finance from private investors and promote environmentally friendly initiatives, without commodifying nature or enabling destructive forms of marine resource exploitation (Voyer et al. 2018). They have engaged in debt-for-climate swaps to enable investments that reduce greenhouse gas emissions and enhance resilience to climate change. These initiatives need to be tailored to each context, but they also need to be scaled up, which will require significant collaboration between bi- and multilateral donors, including, ideally, non-traditional donors (see Hurley et al. 2024). The rechannelling of Special Drawing Rights (SDRs) should be further considered. Cabo Verde, São Tomé and Príncipe, the Maldives, and Jamaica have all taken advantage of funds from the IMF, and other SIDS can potentially benefit (Bishop and Lindsay 2024). Lastly, adopting a more ambitious approach to the current debt, climate, and food crises may form the basis for advocating a new wave of debt forgiveness, providing relief and enabling SIDS to effectively address pressing challenges including climate change, which is the focus of the next section.

4 Small Island Environments

If a permissive liberal order has, for all of its problems, served SIDS reasonably well in terms of economic development, it is not clear whether it will continue to do so, or indeed whether it has produced fewer environmental problems than alternative systems might have. The rise of geopolitical competition between great powers, coupled with the inherent contradictions of global capitalism, is already causing the liberal order to fray, and that is before we even experience the full effects of climate change and biodiversity loss. From the perspective of SIDS, however, climate change threatens to completely overwhelm their development panorama, particularly for those territories – or some of their constituent islands – that are likely to become genuinely uninhabitable. Climate change intersects with the litany of environmental problems that globalisation generates in the form of pollution, pressure on sensitive island ecologies, overdevelopment, excessive reliance on vulnerable coastal zones, and disaster hazards. These combine with other economic and social development challenges, simultaneously aggravating them and requiring resolution if wider solutions are to be found.

SIDS Environments in Historical Context

So far, we have discussed the economic and social history of SIDS in terms of how the conditions and characteristics induced by formal colonialism were reproduced into the independence era. However, this history cannot be divorced from environmental questions. Indeed, the very exploitation of (tropical) islands by colonists was a reflection of both their distinctive physical characteristics and their geographic positioning. This explains why the Caribbean colonial experience – of indigenous genocide, plantation slavery, extractive sugar production, and the establishment of entirely new Creole societies – differed, for the most part, to the Pacific or Indian Ocean equivalent, where more distant, remote, insular societies were not subjected to the same extractive processes in quite the same ways, and pre-existing political structures often endured alongside the implanted colonial order (see Bishop, Corbett, and Veenendaal 2020).

SIDS experienced distinctive patterns of land settlement (and tenure), which in turn shaped how the environment itself would evolve, but many suffered under the exploitative colonial models of plantation agriculture and extractive primary production for export (Barclay et al. 2019). Some have subaerial deposits from past volcanic activity, with hills and steep-sided mountains (Wilkinson et al. 2016). Others are low-lying atolls with the circle-like raised coral at the top of a mountain that is otherwise submerged under the sea. Most SIDS are in tropical climates, enjoy unique flora and fauna and beautiful beaches, making them heavily sought-after holiday destinations (Foley et al. 2023). SIDS are also increasingly referred to as 'large ocean states', a reconceptualisation of their size that emphasises how they occupy often-enormous and resource-rich maritime areas covered by their Exclusive Economic Zones (EEZs) (see Chan 2018).

These 200 nautical miles that extend from their coasts by far exceed their land mass. Thinking about them in this way – as large ocean spaces, rather than small territorial states – also implies that insularity can be beneficial. During the COVID-19 pandemic, such 'splendid isolation' did indeed allow many SIDS to shield themselves against the early spread of the virus (Agius et al. 2022; Connell 2022).

For many SIDS, the coast represents an obvious border – where most of the population, infrastructure, and economic activity is located by the sea, and the sea is visible from much of the interior – shaping psychological conceptions of what it means to be an islander (Bishop and Payne 2012). The same is true of the environment and climate more broadly: people live in unavoidably close proximity to an array of marine and terrestrial animal and plant life, their lives inextricably and viscerally linked to a far greater extent than the urban populations of bigger territories. In short, then, the environment is an integral part of island identity and national policy. Communities have thrived for centuries, despite the threat posed by natural hazards. Locals have relied on rich volcanic soil, a ready food supply, clean water, biodiversity, soil and sand formations, and natural protections from storm surges to survive. SIDS are the global guardians of biodiversity, which holds aesthetic, spiritual, and economic value for their societies.

But long-term survival in many islands is becoming more difficult to envisage because of the intensification of complex patterns of intersecting shocks (Scobie 2019a). SIDS are highly exposed to natural hazards such as hurricanes and cyclones, flooding, drought, and new disease vectors – all of which carry problematic secondary effects – due to their insular tropical location and distinctive topography. Climate change is one of the more relatively recent and pervasive threats, bringing with it troubling challenges linked to sea-level rise, which, in some atolls, is already destroying coastlines. Even for mountainous SIDS, though, it is a pressing concern, because disproportionate concentrations of housing and critical infrastructure – including the most expensive investments, such as airports – are located on the flatter coastal lands, which are themselves limited in scope in territories with small (even tiny) land-to-sea masses (Wilkinson et al. 2016). So, these structures are particularly vulnerable to extreme weather events, and the secondary effects of both immediate shocks and slow-moving challenges like sea-level rise – from saltwater intrusion in delicate and limited freshwater sources to devastating storm surges and beach erosion – continue to accumulate.

These effects are mediated by the distinctive characteristics of individual SIDS, but they all have – to differing degrees – similar patterns of settlement and infrastructural development in coastal areas. Put more crudely: no island can build an airport atop a volcano, and in some, a volcano constitutes as much as 90 per cent of the available land. Around 57 per cent of Pacific Island built infrastructure is located in risk-prone coastal areas (Kumar and Taylor 2015). In Kiribati, the flow of rural populations from outer islands to the low-elevated island of South Tarawa (with a total land area of just $31 km^2$) led to a fourfold increase in the built area located less than 20 m from the shoreline between 1969 and 2008 (Duvat et al. 2013). Maldives also experienced similar recent rural-to-urban migration (Speelman et al. 2016). In the Caribbean, over a decade ago, the cost of climate-related losses was already estimated at \$4bn–\$6bn per annum, or \$187bn by 2080 – in real terms, this number will be much higher today – with water inundation alone likely to decimate almost a third of the region's airports, almost all of its seaports, much of the limited agricultural land that exists, inducing displacement of hundreds of thousands of people (Bishop and Payne 2012: 1544).

Although these effects will play out unevenly, no small island will be immune from them in general, and some, particularly the atoll states, are acutely vulnerable. A significant proportion of land in the Maldives, Marshall Islands, Tuvalu, Kiribati, parts of FSM, and The Bahamas are likely to be uninhabitable under most IPCC scenarios for sea-level rise by 2100 (Oppenheimer et al. 2019). Climate change also contributes to the omnipresent – but less visible, in terms of the global conversation – problem of Sargassum beaching events in the Caribbean, which have rapidly intensified over the past decade and are increasingly devastating for fishing and tourism. This seaweed, which originates in the Atlantic, reaches Caribbean shores in ever-larger volumes because of warming seas, coastal erosion, desertification, and deforestation in the Sahara and South America (Arellano-Verdejo et al. 2019). The region's beaches are inundated with dense mats of the noxious seaweed for several months each year (Almela et al. 2023). Beach clean-ups place a significant financial burden on local tourism and fishers, and are a health concern for local communities.

Global trade – and the pursuit of niche-based development – simultaneously supports and undermines sustainable development in SIDS. On the one hand, it generates exports and much-needed foreign exchange, with 'mass' tourism also necessary for ensuring that metropolitan airlines serve small-island destinations (Bishop 2013). But, on the other, it can drive the progressive loss of biodiversity, exacerbating other environmental stressors. These include overfishing, coral bleaching and reef degradation, water pollution caused by effluent and fertiliser run-off as well as other forms of problematic solid waste management. Indeed, the effect of climate change on biodiversity has been amplified by the heavy dependence of SIDS on large-scale 'mass' tourism (IPBES 2019). Even 'eco' tourism, which, when conducted with sensitivity for local heritage, can be damaging because it also relies on long-haul aviation and can generate unsustainable pressure on the most biodiverse sites – forests, mountains, volcanoes, rural savannahs, farming communities – which host a disproportionate amount of remaining pristine natural patrimony (Bishop 2010). By becoming incorporated into circuits of tourism accumulation, places which were previously relatively isolated can be altered dramatically, both socially and culturally, through their 'green' tourism exploitation.

To note that SIDS have contributed least to the problem of anthropogenic climate change yet suffer an unequal share of both its consequences and the imperative of adapting to it, is, to put it mildly, an understatement. A more radical way of putting it would be that the ongoing accumulation of wealth in those richer countries – and now the 'rising powers' of China, Brazil, and India, as well as many other large polluting states – rests on their continued immiseration through the plundering of a global environmental commons on which small islands rely and have never themselves exploited in terms of their own accumulated historical emissions, but which, as natural capital depletes, is increasingly failing to support the conditions necessary for their continued existence (Sealey-Huggins 2017; Perry 2023; Perry and Sealey-Huggins 2023). Indeed, at the global level, the demands made by SIDS – most notably for restricting global temperature rises to 1.5°C of warming over pre-industrial levels – are likely to be breached in the near future, with some scholars even raising the prospect of 'state extinction' (Vaha 2015).

These trends fuel urgent calls for environmental justice (see Section 5): SIDS have been at the forefront of collective diplomatic efforts to not simply limit warming, but to demand all manner of compensatory mechanisms to both mitigate the worst effects of climate change and facilitate adaptation to them (Mohan 2023). Understandably, SIDS are actively involved in international environmental negotiations through AOSIS, basing their arguments on the notion that they are 'the "canaries in the coalmine" in a tragedy of the commons that is unfolding for all states' (Benwell 2011: 208). They have become powerful norm entrepreneurs, shaping global climate debates and influencing policy, but with mixed success as they face the combined might of the most polluting states (see Betzold 2010; Benwell 2011; Corbett et al. 2019). This builds on a long tradition of SIDS involvement in past oceans negotiations, including the 1982 United Nations Law of the Sea (UNCLOS) Agreement which codified the notion of extensive EEZs.

The point is that while SIDS are not a homogeneous group in terms of their environments any more than their economies or societies, they do face similar challenges to their survival that are amplified by global socio-ecological and economic trends (Popke et al. 2016). This combination of fragility and vulnerability in the context of global environmental change makes their priorities unique. The current permissive order has enabled SIDS to lobby as a unique group of states who share common challenges for collective action across a number of environmental negotiations. This section weighs how environmental and climate governance could play out under the three scenarios addressed in this volume.

Environmental Policy and the Future

A permissive liberal order has, in the environmental sphere, been a double-edged sword for SIDS. It has facilitated the expansion of a global economy driven by the exploitation of fossil fuels, the depletion of natural capital and ever-accreting levels of atmospheric pollution that severely threatens both the biosphere in general and the ongoing development – even existence – of island societies. Yet, at the same time, it is contemporary neoliberal capitalism, which, for all of its problems and pathologies, potentially embodies the requisite technological dynamism through which global decarbonisation and the NetZero transition may occur. Moreover, the voices of SIDS have been amplified and listened to in multilateral climate politics: although this politicking is regularly critiqued for falling short – ambitions watered down, targets missed, funding mechanisms insufficiently replenished, rhetoric belied by inaction – the very fact that fora exist in which island states can pursue their interests, and those interests are taken seriously, being codified in law and materialised (to some degree) in the various climate funds, matters. This is clear if we consider the alternatives.

Scenario One: A Less Liberal and More Competitive, Self-Help Order

As the indicators on the global environmental dashboard continue to flash ever more urgently, and humanity plummets past the planetary boundaries that scientists define as the safe operating spaces for humans and the planet (Rockström et al. 2009), the international response may be a return to a more competitive, self-help system that depends less on elusive international consensus, succumbing to even greater pursuit of self-interest by the powerful. Indeed, unlike the previous sections where the lure of a self-help system tends to come from the right of the political spectrum, in this section the spectre of eco-authoritarianism often comes from the left, where activists are increasingly disillusioned with the ability of a global governance apparatus, created decades ago in a very different context, to secure meaningful emissions reductions in time.

SIDS may benefit from a self-help scenario though. Interstate competition for new technologies potentially opens new areas of economic activity for SIDS that may also steer them away from environmentally and culturally unsustainable large-scale tourism. Such competition could certainly enable low-cost technologies at scale to be deployed by governments to engage in deep-sea mining, renewable energy generation, and harvesting of marine genetic resources. These, in turn, could theoretically help SIDS exploit their large EEZs and expand their 'blue economies' beyond tourism and fishing. The lure of the self-help system is thus especially strong in this section. We think it should be resisted, nonetheless. In the long run it will unavoidably advantage the larger and stronger because SIDS would lose autonomy in shaping policy and the interventions that may directly or indirectly affect their interests (Biermann 2022).

The key to this assessment is our belief that the privileging and prioritisation of domestic concerns in a self-help system would see the dilution of international action and the legal safeguards that protect, for example, their EEZs. This is, after all, how we got into this mess: centuries of self-help by colonists and empires. Fast-forward to the present, and regardless of the best intentions of political leaders and their governments, in a self-help world where treaties lose some (or all) of their force, other malign tendencies become almost inevitable. These include free-riding, where competitor states – and their vested commercial interests – seek to engage in different forms of environmental dumping, whether through explicitly transferring domestic pollution and waste to poorer countries or implicitly debasing their own environmental regulations, which frequently derive from globally agreed standards, to gain an unfair competitive edge (Barnett 2003). This can, in turn, lead to a race-to-the-bottom, which would surely be intensified by the resurgence of pressure from powerful vested interests, especially the fossil fuel lobby. Of course, all of these exist now to a degree: the point is that, under a permissive liberal order, they come into conflict with, and are hemmed in by, functioning multilateral accords that enjoy sufficient support (or acquiescence) and legitimacy (or toleration) to remain operational.

Developing states in general, and SIDS in particular, have never been passive victims of trends towards a competitive self-help order in global environmental governance. Rather, the discourse at the 1972 United Nations Conference on the Human Environment (UNCHE) in Stockholm, even from recently independent states, was that cooperation for environmental stewardship should include attention to the development needs of poorer and more recently independent states. To do otherwise would be to kick away the ladder of industrial growth for those now beginning their climb. Yet it has been clear for some time that, in global climate negotiations, developing country unity – as encompassed in the G77 plus China – masks serious divisions: it is far from obvious that the interests of SIDS are well served by being part of a grouping of states that includes the major Middle Eastern oil producers and the 'rising powers' or 'emerging' BRICS industrial powers (Bishop and Payne 2012). It could even be argued that their interests increasingly intersect with 'Annex 1 countries' – the so-called 'developed countries' signatory to the Paris Agreement – which are most committed to decarbonising agendas. Either way, the key point is that, under a self-help system, the tensions that exist amongst developing countries as a whole would likely result in deep fissures, with the interests of SIDS giving way to those of the BRICS countries and the oil states to an even greater extent than at present.

More broadly, this fragmentation would likely occur alongside the general degradation and delegitimisation of global environmental politics as pursued through the UNFCCC process. So, not only would states with divergent interests be freer to pursue those interests, SIDS would have even fewer means of meaningful redress. As larger states continue with their national environmental policies based purely on their perception of national interest, they will invest fewer resources in more laborious (but less realisable) multilateral solutions. There is a severe risk – even a likelihood – that negotiations would gradually become less ambitious and negotiation blocks more fragmented (Klöck et al. 2022). Any consensus within groupings like the G77 plus China would be unlikely, let alone the agreement of ambitious global accords with legally binding targets. Such fragmentation intrinsically weakens the voices of SIDS in general, but it also means that the issues on which they campaign and in which they have an (existential) interest would become downgraded, especially those pertaining to climate action, loss and damage, climate finance, but also global regulation of overfishing, ocean plastics, and new forms of solar radiation modification (Scobie 2023). For larger states, the appetite, energy, and resources available to address the unique environmental and related economic and societal vulnerabilities of smaller ones are already waning. SIDS may, at best, be abandoned without international assistance at all, or at worst, as during the colonial period and in the Second World War, become the sites for proxy conflicts or scientific testing grounds for larger states, with already-meagre adaptation finance vanishing completely at just the moment they most require it (Lai et al. 2022; Mohan 2023).

A self-help system would also make climate migration trickier. In the absence of meaningful mitigation and adaptation, island peoples will face greater pressure to leave their homes, with migration the sole remaining option for those whose lives and livelihoods are rendered unsustainable by climate change

(Mortreux and Barnett 2009). However, this will coincide with not only an absence of effective international agreement on how, exactly, such migration might be facilitated and governed, but quite plausibly the most restrictive metropolitan immigration regimes conceivable. So, islanders may need to leave, but may also have nowhere at all to go (McLeman 2019). This could create humanitarian crises as territories are lost to the sea or become uninhabitable and as people attempt to reach the metropoles – through irregular routes – and build new lives in them without the requisite protection of formal immigration status (Scobie 2019b).

In sum, while there is a possibility that eco-authoritarianism via self-help could be benevolent, it is unlikely to stay that way for long. And even if it did, a return to a more robust self-help order can deliver neither a restoration of pristine pre-colonial beauty nor the levels of sustainable development that can be envisaged for SIDS under a more permissive order. They would also lose the limited autonomy that they do have in shaping both domestic and international policy pertaining to climate change, and therefore in the interventions that may directly or indirectly affect their interests.

Scenario Two: A More Muscular Liberal Order

A more muscular liberalism, on the other hand, with states working through empowered international institutions and engaging in diplomacy to maximise their collective gains, might more effectively address pressing issues like climate change at the macro level, but possibly in ways that diminish the micro-level space for SIDS to be involved in policymaking, thereby ignoring (even undermining) their specific needs. What this means in practice is that we may see a global accord that drastically reduces carbon emissions and slows down global warming, in turn limiting sea-level rise. But, although this would achieve the greatest aggregate global gains, policies that redound to the individual benefit of SIDS – such as the provision of adaptation finance – could well be downgraded. The likely evaporation of policy space for SIDS reflects the inevitable accretion of power by IOs under intensified liberalism. Indeed, we see elements of this already under the permissive order that is presently decaying: antagonistic states and their politicians perceive that global bodies have simultaneously overreached while failing to deliver the promised aggregate benefits. Of course, one argument for why this is the case could be that multilateral instructions have insufficient autonomy and initiative: they remain stunted by the resistance of powerful states.

All of this helps to explain why global climate agreements are so tortuous to negotiate and why it is so difficult, at present, to envisage a widespread multilateral accord able to both produce and enforce global mitigation that limits warming to 1.5°C. And even were such an order to materialise, powerful states and corporations would still be able to capture the newly empowered IOs – and the wider climate regime – for their own benefit. As before, the most likely form this would take is technification, whereby larger states control narratives around climate remedies and focus on technical fixes rather than radical action and redress (Oye and Maxwell 1994). This has been evident since the earliest 'limits to growth' debates, the exclusion of questions of climate justice from hegemonic policy agendas, and resistance to the need for new and more inclusive forms of cooperation, regulation and governance (Hardin 1968; Feeny et al. 1990; Keohane and Ostrom 1994). The continued quest in international environmental science and policy fora for technocratic solutions to pressing environmental crises, favouring a utilitarian environmentalism that ignores a duty of care to the environment and to the weaker members of the global community, does not augur well for SIDS for whom climate politics should be reshaped around a morality of care, rather than utility (Muradian and Baggethun 2021).

This control by larger states may lead to policies in SIDS that are 'eco-traps', as they attempt to implement global 'conspicuous sustainability' markers that take needed development finance away from other social and developmental needs of their peoples (Grydehøj and Kelman 2017). A more muscular liberalism would also deprive SIDS of effective entry points and levels of engagement, where states and non-state actors influence environmental policy making and outcomes (Green and Auld 2016; Nasiritousi et al. 2016; Abbott 2017; Kuyper et al. 2018). Multi-level governance often leads to competing spaces for agency in decision making (Karlsson-Vinkhuyzen et al. 2022) with non-state actors occupying greater roles than some states in international policy spaces (Chan et al. 2019). In theory, this provides greater scope for influencing the policy process, but it is particularly limiting for SIDS and their civil society organisations, as they do not have the capacity to engage at so many levels of governance (Scobie 2019a).

In sum, a more muscular liberal order may drive technical solutions to environmental crises, but if powerful states prioritise their self-interest over the special and unique needs of SIDS, the solutions sought may be insufficiently targeted. In the best case, increased regulation may bring new institutional forms, discourses, policies and deployment of technologies geared towards global mitigation and remedying (some forms of) environmental degradation. But, this would likely come at a price, restricting policy space, subordinating the interests of SIDS to globally imposed agendas, and forcing them into the eco-traps noted earlier (Grydehøj and Kelman 2017). In the worst case, the compelling claim made by SIDS that they are uniquely deserving of climate justice would be sidelined (Khan et al. 2020) and, consequently, their sovereignty erased either in political discourse or when their islands become submerged under rising sea levels.

Scenario Three: An Enhanced Permissive Liberal International Order

International environmental governance has always been embedded in power politics, with the largest states commonly shaping often-inconsistent narratives, dysfunctional institutions, and sometimes-contradictory laws. It thus remains characterised by 'a significant deficit of ecological integrity' typified by an enduring 'mismatch between rhetoric, intentions and actions' (Stevenson 2021: 86). This disingenuously serves to: elide and enable unsustainable patterns of pollution and resource extraction; dilute commitments on, especially, emissions reductions and phasing out of fossil fuels; and justify failures to meet the attendant targets, especially when it comes to replenishing – and rendering accessible – the various climate funds. This needs to change, urgently, because human activity has had irreversible environmental impacts leading to the 'Anthropocene' era (Grainger 2017; Zalasiewicz et al. 2017), a new geological period requiring novel political solutions to complex environmental crises (Pattberg and Zelli 2016).

SIDS are collectively *the most* vulnerable to accelerating climate change impacts and have been among the most prominent and progressive actors in shaping narratives in international negotiations on climate change (Benwell 2011). They have long championed '1.5 to stay alive' and are among the most vocal on 'loss and damage' debates. For this reason, we suggest that a more permissive liberal order will allow the voice of SIDS to be amplified, rather than side-lined as would be the case in the previous two scenarios. A more permissive liberal order provides SIDS with the discursive space, platforms, and institutions to galvanise norms like climate justice and intergenerational equity that support their interests. At present, we are actually witnessing two countervailing trends. On the one hand, elements of a robust and more muscular liberalism can be seen in an exclusionary, but ever-expanding, climate regime that generates binding mitigation-focused targets that remain insufficient to slow down the accelerating pace of global heating, while producing important, but nevertheless poorly resourced, mechanisms that are unable to effectively support adaptation efforts in SIDS. On the other, elements of a self-help system are also evident in the ways that powerful states regularly – almost systematically – abrogate the commitments made under the regime, while engaging in a technological arms race, deploying the kinds of aggressive subsidies that were inconceivable under the permissive neoliberal order, to gain competitive advantage in the 'green' sectors of the future.

In light of this, the possibility that a more permissive order could be possible appears to take on heroic proportions because statist tendencies coexist and conflict so obviously with liberal globalist ones, making it difficult to imagine them in productive tension. Today, global environmental governance is arguably premised on a distinctive form of liberal environmentalism (Bernstein 2002) that was based on economic rationality, deregulation and self-regulation by private actors, environmental steering by experts, and market mechanisms to manage environmental issues (Mayrand 2020). This order recognised the norms of sustainable development and created important global environmental architectures, including the 1992 Rio Declaration on Environment and Development, the 1992 Convention on Biological Diversity and the 1992 UNFCCC (Tallberg 2020). A more permissive liberalism would allow for the involvement of more actors, including non-state actors and indigenous communities, which may in turn further the agendas of SIDS (Chan 2021). But it would inevitably be more complicated, making it harder to reach consensus.

Yet, outside of the international negotiations space, the permissive liberal order offers SIDS a range of global to local processes, forums, programmes, actors, and agents with the capability and autonomy to support their agendas (Scobie 2023). While SIDS continue to lobby for support for their environmental resilience from the historic environment debtors, they simultaneously leverage coalitions of more powerful states (Sikkink 2014), youth movements (Feldman 2021), academia, the media (Jaschik 2014), scientists, public–private partnerships (Pattberg 2010; Burch et al. 2013), and even international processes that do not have direct environmental remits. For example, they engage with those able to provide expertise and support for programmes of community-based adaptation (Mercer, Kelman, and Mavrogenis 2014). The rights of climate migrants may also be taken up outside of processes like the UNFCCC. Islanders often argue that their concerns should not only serve to legitimise northern frames around their plight (often painting them as passive victims). Rather, a more permissive liberal order provides space for alternative framings, for example, approaching climate change as a human rights issue, and climate migration from SIDS as a proactive step and dignified, conscious choice (Tanja and Voyer 2015; Scobie 2019b).

A more permissive order would also enable SIDS to continue to call for environmental justice through international law and diplomacy. Vanuatu has set this in motion, bringing a vote to the United Nations General Assembly (UNGA) on 29 March 2023, and the successful adoption of a resolution requesting an advisory opinion from the International Court of Justice (ICJ) on the obligations of States with respect to climate change. This opinion could prove a critical watershed moment in supporting the positions of SIDS and other climate-vulnerable countries in climate negotiations (Wewerinke-Singh and Salili 2020; Wilkinson et al. 2022). Although not binding on states, the strength of its legal arguments will carry great weight and could open the door for rights-based climate litigation in domestic courts around the world.

In sum, an enhanced permissive liberal order is likely to provide more opportunities for SIDS than the two alternatives on offer. It would reinvigorate global multilateralism in ways that increase the capacity of island states to set the terms of debate, make their own demands of global institutions and funding mechanisms, while eschewing the disempowering one-size-fits-all nature of a more muscular liberalism. It would also resist some of the malign tendencies of a statist self-help system, constraining the ability of more powerful states to soft-defect – that is, to implicitly neglect or even explicitly disregard their international obligations – to the same extent as at present, incentivising them to meet their financial and other commitments to others, increasing compliance costs and encouraging burden-sharing (especially in green technology). Although SIDS will struggle to push the historic emitters (and rising powers) further than they wish to go on reductions, the diversity inherent in a permissive liberal order means that other alliances are available outside of dedicated international forums like the UNFCCC, which can help SIDS face these head-winds and in some cases even champion their environmental causes.

Towards a More Permissive Liberal International Order

There is now sustained transnational mobilisation around 'environmental racism', 'ecocide', and 'climate justice' emphasising the essentially discriminatory and unequal burden borne by the Global South, not only in terms of relative historical greenhouse gas emissions, but also the extent to which industrialisation in the Global North rested on colonial plunder and neocolonial resource extraction and, today, reinforces the trajectory of global heating, thereby restricting the policy space of formerly colonised societies to engage in similar forms of polluting development. A successful NetZero transition in the Global North may, of course, alter this calculation, but, even so, without meaningful technology transfer, it could also impose new costs on poorer countries as richer ones redeploy the development gains of the past to re-industrialise and capture emerging 'green' sectors. Either way, demands for climate justice, and the already-existing movements that have mobilised around them, may provide the ideological building blocks for a repurposed international order that allows groups like SIDS to have greater leverage in global environmental politics (Almeida 2019).

Prioritising their needs and participation in the governance of, and policymaking in, multilateral climate funds is crucial. At the time of writing, twenty-eight SIDS have fully costed Nationally Determined Contributions (NDCs), amounting to \$287 billion over the next decade. Yet while they are considered 'particularly vulnerable' by the Global Climate Fund (GCF) and other vertical climate funds, SIDS face significant barriers to accessing the requisite finance (see Wilkinson et al. 2023b). They receive significantly less climate finance when compared with LDCs and other groups of countries (Wilkinson et al. 2023). They have high transaction costs because of their geographical remoteness and limited economies of scale, and this is amplified by their archipelagic nature: building the necessary regional infrastructures to offset small size is difficult everywhere, even in the Caribbean where islands are reasonably close to each other (Bishop and Payne 2010; Bishop et al. 2021a). The same is true in individual archipelago states – especially in the Pacific and Indian Ocean – where small populations are spread over vast ocean distances. Take Kiribati: the only country on earth to straddle all four hemispheres, consisting of 33 atolls and islands – of which 22 are inhabited with 129,000 people – comprising just 811km^2 of land distributed across 3.44 *million* km^2 of sea, a distance of 3,900 km from east to west and 2,100 km from north to south. An extreme example, to be sure, but not an unusual one. The use of 'beneficiary metrics' by the GCF that assess project costs on per-person benefits is disadvantageous to SIDS since the already-higher transaction costs are spread among often-tiny populations (Wilkinson et al. 2023b). Improved governance of these funds would require more consultative and inclusive decentralised programming and decision-making that are sensitive to the perspectives and concerns of local stakeholders in each SIDS region. This will help the project evaluators to better understand the costs, capacities, and constraints of SIDS in their climate action endeavours.

More broadly, a better alignment between the sources of climate financing for adaptation, environmental protection, and ecosystem restoration would help SIDS. Funds have different mandates, donors, metrics, and fiduciary requirements, often viewing small islands as too small to invest in, while the latter's ministries and climate departments have minimal capacity, consequently struggling with the multiplicity of arduous application and reporting templates required from each project funder (Bishop et al. 2023). Access and reporting requirements frequently have inaccurate assumptions about state capacity when SIDS and regional partners are absent in the co-design of projects. Multi-island programmes and more programmatic finance may help SIDS build capacity over the medium- to long-term (CFAN 2023). The experience of some Pacific countries during the COVID-19 pandemic, where direct budget support from donors was put to good use, is instructive.

The key point is that if SIDS continue to be viewed as legitimate members of an international community predicated on norms of sovereign equality and rights to development, and, crucially, survival, then it is for the climate funds and MDBs to instigate changes in their operating practices to better accommodate their needs and properly serve their interests, not the other way around. This kind of reform – piecemeal as it often may be – and progress on the agendas favoured by SIDS, such as capitalisation of the Loss and Damage Fund, are more likely under a permissive liberal order. Indeed, the very fact that the fund was established, in 2022, is strong evidence of progress achieved under the existing system. However, for these agendas to move forward, island states need to continue to win the normative battle: highlighting their incommensurate lack of historic responsibility for climate change; the existential threat its acceleration poses for their societies; their desperate need for a reduction in greenhouse gas emissions which is proceeding too slowly despite soaking up an excessive share of pooled resources, the pace or extent of which they cannot (and have no responsibility to) influence; the urgency of their attendant need to adapt to the imposed harm of climate change, an imperative for which the relative resources available are smaller, insufficient, and difficult to access; and the ongoing need to cover permanent losses and damages with those contributions, and other forms of development assistance, predicated on justice, not gratuity.

5 Small Island Diplomacy

The state is the fundamental building block of IR theory. Realists classically view conflict between self-interested states as the inexorable outcome of power imbalances in an anarchic international system. Liberals counter that cooperation can mitigate anarchy and provide the public good of order, attenuating disorder. Each position, at the extreme, reflects the two outlier scenarios – self-help vs muscular liberalism – discussed in this Element. Mainstream scholars and policymakers worry about the breakdown of liberal order precisely because the imbalance of power that has followed the waning of US hegemony – which underpinned the post-1945 'embedded liberal' and post-1970s 'neoliberal' variants of this order – may generate greater conflict (Ikenberry 2008). But whether unipolar or multipolar, the principle of sovereign equality is a foundational norm of the post–Second World War order, despite the fact that all states are different. Much IR theory revolves around these differences: that is, explaining the ways 'great' powers determine the form and function of the international system while 'middle' powers and 'small' states have less influence on the basis of their size, wealth or military capacity (Vital 1967, 1971). The implication is that, the smaller the state, the less relevant it is, with SIDS having negligible influence or significance. Waltz (1979: 97) famously argued that it would be 'ridiculous to construct a theory of international politics based on Malaysia and Costa Rica'. Yet smaller countries have – and continue to have – a level of diplomatic influence that belies their diminutive stature. This section explains why that matters.

SIDS Diplomacy in Historical Context

Waltz was writing his *Theory of International Politics*, the foundational treatise of neo-Realist IR, at the exact moment that many of the very smallest micro-states were becoming independent. However, these countries have not simply survived politically, but in many cases thrived, shaping the contours of regional and international politics in important ways. The same is true of countries like Malaysia and Costa Rica, with populations of thirty million and five million respectively. Indeed, the latter has generated the most successful economy and peaceful society in Central America despite (or perhaps because of) not having a military. This matters, because for classical realists military strength is the essence of power in an anarchic state system. By implication, the fact that SIDS have thrived beyond decolonisation demonstrates *how* permissive the order has become. Indeed, we can only imagine what Waltz would think of the idea that Tuvalu – with a population of 11,000, GDP per capita of around USD5,500, and also without a military – might be able to survive as a state, let alone influence world affairs.

Mainstream IR theory therefore has very little to tell us about SIDS: it cannot explain *why* they have been able to develop distinctive foreign policies that have delivered more than mere survival; *how* the international system enables or constrains their often-high levels of development; *where* they have been able to contest, sometimes with great success, the preferences of bigger players; or *when* this action has led to the creation and shaping of new norms that have influenced important areas of international policy (see Ingebritsen et al. 2012). They have instead been identified as little more than oddities that exist as a consequence of 'America's crusading spirit' (Keohane 1969). However, on the margins of the discipline, and among small state scholars in particular, there exists a considerably more nuanced and sophisticated discussion of their cap-acity to influence the world system (Baldacchino 2023). Indeed, some scholars have gone so far as to argue that they have been engaged in 'worldmaking' (Getachew 2019) since the Second World War, and thus the order is, to some extent, 'adapted' to their needs. We need not go quite that far in this Element. But we do start from an analogous position that considers SIDS as 'subjects, not objects' in international diplomacy (Neumann and Gstöhl 2006). Recognising this offers considerable scope to imagine how they might continue to alter the international order for their own benefit.

The first strand of IR theory that takes SIDS seriously accepts the materialist assumption that size, in a broad sense, determines outcomes (see Pedi and Wivel 2023). The claim here is that all states have an 'action space' or a point at which their capacities and system-determining effects intersect. This action space is contingent on size, however defined, which can explain why larger states, with greater capacity, can exert a proportionate influence on international affairs. Yet smaller states can still act – they are not passive recipients whatever large states decree – albeit their actions are circumscribed to a much greater extent by a system created by great powers. Small states thus have to pursue 'smart' strategies and policy 'entrepreneurship' to achieve their goals (e.g. Browning 2006; Grøn and Wivel 2011). Much work in this vein has been developed in Europe and in EU studies in particular to explain the foreign policy agendas and outcomes of the majority of smaller countries in that region (Thorhallsson 2017; Panke 2010). But these lessons can be applied to SIDS, too.

The second strand is a 'relational' approach. Rather than emphasising vulnerabilities, this 'recognises the importance of material capabilities, perceptions, and positionality' (Long 2022: 15). However, it does not assume that these phenomena *determine* outcomes in a mechanistic fashion. Rather, scholars working from a relational perspective argue that we should focus on interactions between states, whatever their size, because it is the asymmetry that matters. Put differently: outcomes cannot only be reduced to size and material power, as relationships, diplomacy, perceptions of shared interests, and so on are important, too. Small states can persuade larger ones to support initiatives that do not redound to the latter's private benefit because of a perception that they may augment the stock of collective public goods so that everyone benefits. So, for example, even though neither the US nor Australia is as small as Tuvalu, the relationship between them is defined by asymmetry, which has consequences for explaining their foreign policy. The implications are twofold: size matters and 'there is no single recipe for small states' foreign policy success' (Long 2022: 178).

The third approach argues that perceptions of shared interests may not only influence (asymmetric) outcomes from diplomacy, but the very intersubjective understandings that underpin the international system and practice within it can be redefined and reshaped by the norm entrepreneurship of small-island actors, which in turn generates significant material outcomes that belie their diminutive size. Their lack of conventional power resources can even represent a resource itself, rather than a constraint, enabling action precisely because they can fly under the radar, using their powers of moral suasion, guile, and nimbleness to engage in unorthodox system-influencing behaviour. To understand the influence of a state, then, we have to uncover how their leaders (and other elites) perceive the order, its constituent norms, their meaning and significance, and the choices that this presents, so as to explain actions and outcomes.

The key idea we take for SIDS from this ideational approach, and the one on which this Element turns, is that balancing the norms of a right to development, sovereignty equality, and non-intervention renders the liberal order permissive of small states. Again, as Sharman (2017: 560) argues, the irrelevance of military threats to statehood, combined with the safety net provided by foreign aid, suggests that 'the current international system presents even its smallest and weakest members with choices rather than imperatives'. To be clear, small states do not have everything their own way: evidently, international politics still broadly reflects the preferences of the most powerful. Structure and agency remain co-constituted: actors and their decisions are always 'situated' in specific contexts. But, the key point is that SIDS *are* subjects that can act meaningfully with intention and deploy normative power, not objects whose behaviour is pre-determined solely by material inequality or asymmetric bargaining. This can explain why, for example, some small island communities have opted to decolonise via independence and have since pursued non-alignment. Others prefer forms of non-sovereignty or have aligned their diplomatic efforts to those of larger states. A diversity of options is open to leaders from SIDS precisely because they created a system of norms that recognise and protect diversity. The key for their survival at this moment of change is that this diversity is valued into the future.

International Alliances and the Future

A permissive order has not only given SIDS a seat at the table, it has, by codifying their sovereign equality, offered them a framework of laws, regulations, norms and practices through which they might deploy their sovereignty as a resource that produces meaningful outcomes, even wielding disproportionate governing power in some policy arenas (see Bishop and Cooper 2018). Although they have fought many losing battles, and frequently been sidelined from some corridors of power – whether overtly, as in their exclusion from bodies such as the G20, or implicitly, by a lack of capacity to participate in processes driven by elite consensus (Payne 2010; Bishop and Payne 2021b) – the very fact that they have been able to play the game in the first place is remarkable. Yet as the permissive order that facilitated this decays, the alternative scenarios appear rather bleak.

Scenario One: A Less Liberal and More Competitive, Self-Help System

The key geopolitical shift over the last decade is the rise of China as a genuine challenger to US hegemony. The scale of this transformation, which appears obvious today, was barely anticipated at the turn of the millennium, with the Chinese economy *trebling* in size during the intervening period, an industrial revolution that took up to a century in the West (Bishop 2016, 2018). China's growing influence has been met with increasing anxiety by the US and its allies, especially in a post-global financial crisis context in which their own economies are faltering and appear to be beset by deep, immutable structural problems that impede growth. After a long period of market opening, this has coincided with Xi's authoritarian turn (Shirk 2018) and removal of term limits. Consequently, western policymakers not only worry about China's growing confidence and international assertiveness, they fear that its successful blending of intensified authoritarianism *and* developmentalism offers an unfavourable contrast to stagnating market liberalism (Bishop 2018, 2022).

This, in turn, has two troubling effects. First, it potentially gives succour to western 'anti-system' actors like Trump and others seeking to transcend the neoliberal era by doubling down on its most malign aspects while simultaneously emulating those authoritarian tendencies and unpicking the multilateral settlement (Hopkin 2020). Second, the US and its allies are increasingly concerned that they will be overwhelmed by an economic model that they cannot keep pace with, and which has already provoked premature deindustrialisation in even major developing countries to the extent that they appear increasingly unable to compete in global markets that Chinese capital has, because of its sheer scale, come to dominate (Muzaka 2017; Hopewell 2019, 2020). The consequence is that, since the COVID-19 shock began to subside, the US, the EU, and China have become locked in a competitive developmentalist race to subsidise and nurture next-generation industrial sectors (Lavery 2024). This form of state capitalism is quite different from the market liberalism that typified the permissive era (Alami and Dixon 2024).

Obviously, the US itself has violated the norms of the liberal order over many decades, with perceived interests frequently trumping moral consistency. This lends support to the realist contention that, when push comes to shove, power and might always trump shared values. However, as liberals such as Ikenberry (2008) have argued, a key difference is that, because, historically, the US and its allies are democracies, violations of international norms were met with domestic censure and political opposition. This may be nothing more than 'organised hypocrisy' (Krasner 1999). But the point is that at least the hypocrisy acts as a handbrake on the exercise of unilateral power.

Whether that will continue to be the case is an open question, especially in light of Trump's presidency, continued hyper-partisanship in US politics, and the erosion of the twentieth-century media model across democratic nations grappling with the 'post-truth' era.

In the short term, the escalation of great power competition appears to be having both positive and negative impacts for SIDS. The positive effect is that heightened geopolitical competition has brought SIDS attention from great powers, and this has in turn led to increased resources. Previously, as the scholar and former Prime Minister of St Lucia Vaughan Lewis (2009: vii) noted, large states, like their cadres of realist academics, have typically viewed small states as little more than 'irritants in international relations' (see also Vital 1967, 1971). They had limited strategic or economic value, but required high levels of ODA, especially in the Pacific, and struggled to translate this into developmental gains. The upshot is that they appeared to be a never-ending sink for funds that generated few, if any, returns, either in economic, strategic, or diplomatic terms. Climate change altered this calculation to some extent because it led to SIDS acting as a bloc in international organisations, and the rise of China has completely upended the older view. Now, SIDS, especially in the Pacific, are being extensively courted by both China and the US and its allies.

SIDS are no strangers to donor shopping because China and Taiwan have been engaged in a struggle for diplomatic recognition for decades. At the time of writing, Belize, Haiti, Marshall Islands, Palau, Saint Kitts and Nevis, Saint Lucia, St Vincent and the Grenadines, and Tuvalu all recognised Taiwan. But these numbers have fluctuated over the years: Guyana established diplomatic relations with Taiwan, but suddenly reversed its decision after China intervened, and St Lucia has switched between the two more than once. In the Pacific, Solomon Islands, Kiribati, and Nauru have all made the 'switch' to China in recent years. The difference today is the scale and the forms of leverage that SIDS can now generate (Wallis et al. 2023). In 2022, for example, China signed a security co-operation agreement with Solomon Islands that sent shockwaves across the Pacific and rattled the US and its allies who had assumed that a recent, decades-long multibillion dollar Australian-led intervention to restore stability in the country would have gained them greater influence. The fact that it did not, and that Solomon Islands was prepared to look after its own developmental needs irrespective of Australia's wishes, had not been factored into the strategic calculations of larger states. China subsequently failed to sign a regional agreement with other Pacific states, and the diplomatic response from the US and its allies was swift, and included increased aid. But if anything, the bidding war confirms how much the geopolitical game has changed and highlights the different options SIDS now have at their disposal to generate the assistance they need.

The longer-term consequences of this shift are likely to be less attractive to SIDS. In the extreme, rising tensions could lead to military conflict in which they become embroiled despite having little stake in the outcomes. This is the lesson of the Second World War when Pacific SIDS, in particular, were sites upon which armed conflict occurred, with detrimental impacts to their communities and environment, the effects of which can still be seen on Guadalcanal, Tarawa, Kwajalein, Chuuk, and Peleliu, to name a few of the more infamous battles. Moreover, Pacific SIDS, in particular, but also some other non-sovereign Caribbean territories – notably the Puerto Rican island of Vieques – have long been sites of weapons testing, both during and after the Cold War. The US legacy in the Marshall Islands is the most devastating, but the UK and France have also tested weapons in the region. In all cases, communities and their islands have been severely impacted. The US also continues to rent Kwajalein as a base for intercontinental missile testing and has recently signed an agreement to establish a military facility in FSM; while Guam, which is part of the US, is one of Washington's most important strategic bases in the Asia-Pacific region. A similar story could be told about the Chagos Islanders whose right to return home from Mauritius to the British Indian Ocean Territory, which hosts the Diego Garcia base, has been continually denied despite winning repeated international legal victories affirming it.

Even if rising geopolitical tensions only simmer at Cold War–type levels, the strategic location of SIDS is likely to see their autonomy eroded, perhaps substantially. Caribbean countries have already been subjected to a mild version of this over recent decades due to the US-led war on drugs, which led to increased US surveillance and policing in their territory through such mechanisms as the Shiprider Agreement (see Griffith 1997; Bishop and Kerrigan 2023). The potential for considerably more invasive and controlling relationships with larger states is significant. Ideas about suzerainty and vassalage have a long history in European political thought. It is not too much of a stretch to imagine that China might be interested in establishing similar relationships, too. Indeed, the prospect of this occurring was an underlying fear for the US and its allies when Solomon Islands signed its security agreement with Beijing. More generally, one lesson from the 'Age of Empire' for SIDS is that an illiberal, self-help order is likely to see the larger annex the smaller, regardless of their consent.

Scenario Two: A More Muscular Liberal Order

In light of the existential threat that an illiberal order poses for SIDS, it is tempting to argue that the scenario they ought to favour and pursue is one in which liberal norms and values are asserted in a more muscular fashion, with the US remaining ascendant and re-embracing its core democratic values, supported by acquiescent like-minded partners such as the EU, Japan, the UK, and other democratic states. In this scenario, the state is superseded by drastically empowered multilateral institutions, both regional and global, and an expanded corpus of international law, which sets and enforces the rules of the game in which all states, including SIDS, operate. Although aspects of this scenario are attractive to SIDS, especially as many of them are liberal democratic states, to our mind it also has significant potential to increase interventionism – albeit from distant technocrats, rather than belligerent states – and flatten diversity in the pursuit of standardisation, whether to facilitate trade, uphold rights, or pursue other globally mandated objectives.

Multilateral institutions, be they international or regional, could step in and coordinate activities for SIDS, leading to improved development outcomes. But the danger is that multilateral institutions often compound their problems and – in a context where their choices are already constrained – lead to further diminished autonomy and independence of policymaking. Indeed, a more muscular liberalism, by definition, would imply circumscribed sovereignty (for all states) as the price of delivering public goods. But SIDS would suffer most: they already experience asymmetry directly when dealing with development banks, such as the World Bank Group (WBG) and the IMF, in particular, but also bilateral donors. The MDBs have tended to make loans conditional on reducing the size of the bureaucracy, especially during economic and fiscal crises. Bilateral donors have also focused heavily on improving governance, as well as advancing gender issues and human rights. Both presume that SIDS are responsible for their economic problems, regardless of colonial legacies or instances where they have suffered the collateral damage from decisions by larger states – as we saw in previous sections with the shift from the GATT to the WTO – as well as climate-induced shocks. At the same time, though, SIDS have struggled to generate the same level of influence in these economic IOs, many of which have rules and procedures, including weighted, group-based voting that favours larger states, than they have in the realm of climate diplomacy.

The dominant pattern noted earlier could become considerably worse in a more muscular liberal order, with the norm of non-interference giving way to an international regime that prioritised good governance, human rights, and developmental needs irrespective of the wishes of democratically elected governments. Indeed, such tensions are already apparent in some SIDS over social policy issues such as gender equality, gay marriage, carceral practices, and capital punishment. They are also latent in opposition to global economic integration that is seen to restrict policy space through what the Jamaican intellectual Norman Girvan (2010) once described as an anti-democratic elite process of 'technification' (rendering policy issues incomprehensible to, and therefore incontestable by, the public), 'sweetification' (offering short-term financial inducements to secure damaging long-term structural adjustments), and 'treatyfication' (hemming states in to an ever-expanding corpus of regulatory constraints).

The upshot is that a more muscular liberalism could be attractive in the same way that donor shopping provides advantages for SIDS. It could, in theory, lead to all manner of expanded global public goods such as stronger human rights protections. But in practice, it also has the potential to deliver significant downsides because it would likely see the erosion of the norm of non-interference in the name of the right to development, which in the long run would increase the perception among SIDS that their future is no longer theirs to control. It could also sow the seeds of its own destruction: if a liberal order were to realise its full promise – an unimaginable redistribution of global power away from the largest states and up to the global level in order to deliver an array of public goods – it is highly likely that large states would revolt. It is, then, unimaginable in both senses of the word: not just difficult to envision, but potentially inconceivable, too.

Scenario Three: An Enhanced Permissive Liberal International Order

As outlined, a permissive order in which SIDS are able to balance norms of sovereign equality, non-interference, and the right to development is most likely to provide them with 'choices rather than imperatives' (Sharman 2017: 560). The third scenario would therefore involve the continuation, repair, and enhancement of the post–Second World War order and the advantages it wrought for SIDS, especially via their membership of IOs. We can see the potential of this permissiveness most clearly in the ways that SIDS have positioned themselves in climate negotiations, including via AOSIS (see Betzold 2010; Klöck 2020). Here, when working as a bloc, SIDS have collectively created and utilised key mechanisms – including the categorisation of 'SIDS' itself, the decennial UNSIDS conferences, and the COP processes – to advance their agenda. This has led to widespread recognition of their vulnerabilities to climate impacts, and, as of COP27, the potential to achieve climate justice via the establishment of a loss and damage fund.

SIDS were active in the creation of the post–Second World War order via the decolonisation process. Early decolonial thinking, for example, followed the 'largeness is strength' model. Small islands, both at home and abroad, were widely considered to have limited development prospects and were likely to be easily manipulated by foreign powers, especially in the context of the Cold War. Yet the independence of countries such as Barbados, Jamaica, Samoa, Trinidad and Tobago, Malta (classified as a SIDS until 2004 when it acceded to the EU), Nauru, and Cook Islands during the 1960s recast this model and demonstrated that size was no barrier to the exercise of sovereignty. While not all communities followed, these early examples precipitated a boom in small stateness during the 1970s and 1980s, shrinking the average size of the state globally in the process. Each was then recognised, by IOs like the UN, which reaffirmed the principles of sovereign equality and non-interference as foundational norms irrespective of state size and the capacity of communities to exercise their viability via military or economic means.

At the same time, in the early independence period, these new small states struggled to impose their foreign policy agendas on the international system. As naysayers predicted, size-related asymmetries, including their small foreign ministries and limited domestic bureaucratic capacity, made it hard for them to develop and pursue independent foreign policy agendas. Domestic growth and development remained limited – with many larger SIDS, particularly those dependent on agricultural and other primary product exports, suffering relative economic decline due to declining terms of trade through the commodity shocks of the 1970s – until the explosion of the tourism and financial services sectors in the late 1980s and early 1990s. Regional integration, the often-cited panacea to the myriad problems faced by SIDS, stalled in the face of persistent island and communal nationalism. And the Commonwealth, the one institution which is dominated by SIDS and therefore should be capable of advancing their interests – and had undertaken much of the early definitional and analytical work conceptualising their distinctive panorama of vulnerability – was increasingly struggling for relevance and funding. In this milieu, observers reflected that some SIDS, such as Tuvalu, were 'prisoners of their independence' (Crocombe 2008: 418)

Yet it is the very recognition of this vulnerability that has, ironically, proven to be a strength in an order that was rhetorically committed to the idea that all states should have an equal right to development (Corbett et al. 2019). Co-ordinated by AOSIS, the countries we now call SIDS enshrined their vulnerability in the 1992 Rio Earth Summit conference, embedded it and the SIDS category in the international system at the first UNSIDS conference in 1994, spread their agenda across IOs in the subsequent decade, and played a key role in pushing ambitious climate targets, including most famously via the Paris Agreement in 2015. They have also co-ordinated positions and worked via larger groupings in IOs, including the Non-Aligned Movement, the G77 plus China, the UN Group of Latin American and Caribbean Countries (GRULAC), friends of SIDS, and others. Some of the very smallest SIDS have chaired the UN General Assembly and served as non-permanent members of the Security Council, and their diplomatic corps have been renowned for their skill at coalition-building – often constructing bridges between the Global North and South – and exercising norm entrepreneurship on 'low politics' issues that have enduring significance. As the Guyanese diplomat, Rudy Insanally (2012) once put it, small states are masters of the art of 'letting others have your way'.

The success of these efforts, and the idea that vulnerability could be a strength – even if its rhetorical acceptance has not, as yet, unlocked material gains as a basis for ODA, concessional finance or SDT – still remain the best evidence that we have of how permissive the post–Second World War order has been. SIDS have, though, not had everything their own way. As alluded to elsewhere, they have struggled to translate their influence in climate discussions into similar advantages in economic IOs. Even in climate discussions, they have suffered from 'bandwagoning' in which larger states generate favourable publicity by association, but once the set-piece events are over, their commitments fail to eventuate. Moreover, by creating difficult-to-overcome bureaucratic hurdles in order to access international funds, they have made it so difficult for SIDS that finance does not flow to them despite their disproportionate need (Wilkinson et al. 2023b). Over time, tensions have also appeared within AOSIS itself, whose cross-regional breadth is a strength in terms of negotiating power but a limitation in terms of coordinating positions, especially given the distances (and time zones) that separate island capitals. Linguistic differences have also meant that the SIDS agenda largely remains dominated by anglophone countries.

But, putting these limitations to one side, the success of SIDS over the last three decades is further proof that a permissive order presents important advantages relative to the main alternatives discussed earlier. The reason is that the tension between the norms of sovereign equality, non-interference, and the right to development enables SIDS to turn their vulnerability into a strength. In doing so, they have inverted the common international relations hierarchy in which large is perceived irredeemably to be better than small.

Towards a More Permissive Liberal International Order

Any move to make the order drastically less or more liberal is likely to see key norms that have advantaged SIDS – sovereign equality, non-interference, and the right to development – undermined. Their main foreign policy objective, as individual states and groups, must therefore involve ensuring those norms are maintained, even though they are often in tension and produce forms of 'organised hypocrisy'. In pursuing this objective, it is important to be mindful of the factors that SIDS have used to secure successes in the past (see especially Corbett et al. 2021; Baldacchino 2023). Specifically, they have realised their objectives when they have been able to coordinate global positions – rather than being siloed into regions – and maintain an active diplomatic presence in the cities where the major IOs are located, predominantly New York and Geneva. This presence and global coordination has been facilitated by organisations like AOSIS and initiatives like the Commonwealth Small States offices in both cities. But it also relies on SIDS governments themselves prioritising diplomacy via multilateral institutions.

Existing efforts to pursue foreign policy objectives in this way have had most success in the UN system and on environmental issues. SIDS have, as noted, been less successful in economic IOs such as the WTO and the MDBs (Corbett et al. 2021). But the principle – that when institutional spaces are created by and for SIDS they are able to maximise them to secure advantages and alleviate their condition – which worked for them in the UN system is applicable to these IOs, too. We therefore advocate for MDB reform in particular as a practical example of how SIDS can ensure the current order becomes more permissive of their presence. This is a priority for all developing countries; but for SIDS, there is a huge amount at stake and they should have a louder voice in this agenda. In particular, the G20 Experts Group on Strengthening the MDBs called for a tripling of MDB financing, the inclusion of global public goods in their formal mission statements, and a new window for funding those programmes. These are critical agendas for SIDS. Dedicated support for global public goods is particularly important for them too as custodians of large EEZs and high levels of biodiversity, for which they are not currently being adequately compensated. SIDS should therefore advocate strongly for concrete action on the World Bank's new vision to 'create a world free of poverty – on a liveable planet.'

The 'Bridgetown Initiative', launched by Barbadian Prime Minister Mottley during the 2022 UNGA meetings, called for significant increases in access to finance for vulnerable developing countries, including through SDR re-allocations and changes to the global debt management architecture, including wider use of debt pause clauses. Progress is being made on both these issues, but SIDS as a group need to engage more concertedly with this agenda to ensure the results meet their needs and do not end up increasing the costs of borrowing. Other proposed reforms, such as on capital adequacy (encouraging MDBs to unlock more capital) and mobilising private finance for development, are also important for SIDS across all income categories. More finance is needed for them to build resilient economies, but their demands will continue to face opposition from other larger developing countries unless the pot of resources can be increased. On MDB reform, as with other advocacy agendas, SIDS will do better if they stand together, but will also need to connect with, and support, demands and voices from across the G77 plus China group if their special circumstances and priorities are to be meaningfully recognised. MDBs must also acknowledge the importance of traditional knowledge and culture in social and development programmes, meaning greater flexibility and localisation of interventions, as opposed to the neoliberal tendency of ready-made policies and strategies with externally imposed conditionalities.

Conclusion: Towards a More Permissive Liberal Order

Social scientists cannot predict the future, but some try. Researchers working in a 'naturalist' tradition seek to make *social* science more 'scientific' (as if wearing lab coats and protective glasses). Yet laws that are equivalent to those in the physical sciences, such as gravity, are nowhere to be found in the human world. Society itself, like the theories we build to comprehend it, is a human construct. It exists in the meanings and perceptions attached to relationships, events and processes – what we have called norms – which help us make sense of the world around us. Consequently, the best that scholars can do is attempt to understand these meanings to explain action, and, hopefully, provide a map that can guide and rationalise responses from those with the power to influence policy. In this Element, we have attempted to explain why SIDS appear to have come to a fork in the road in which the developmental gains achieved during the latter half of the twentieth century, in particular, appear to be slipping away. We conclude by restating why we believe that this is happening, defending our explanation against anticipated criticisms, and summarising what might be done to forge a more prosperous future.

Our Argument Summarised

We make three central claims in this Element. First, contrary to prevailing wisdom at the time – a predominant view that we generally shared – many SIDS made substantial development gains during the 1990s and 2000s as they transitioned from post-colonial preference-based agriculture and into niche services attendant with the high point of neoliberal globalisation. To be sure, these were unevenly spread, within and between island states, and certainly volatile, reflecting both the essential capriciousness of often-enclave sectors that depend on unrestricted flows of capital and the dependent position of SIDS within the wider global political economy. Indeed, when the global financial crisis struck in 2008, it highlighted not only the scale of exposure faced by highly open small economies when a massive shock arrives, but also how this is exacerbated by reliance on globally integrated sectors like tourism and offshore finance. The arrival of a second 'once in a generation' shock just over a decade later – the COVID-19 pandemic – which again halted tourism completely, reinforced this lesson. It also bookended a period of Gramscian 'interregnum' where neoliberalism has been engulfed by a legitimacy crisis while 'morbid symptoms' have proliferated (see Bishop and Payne 2021a).

Second, the gains enjoyed by SIDS rested on a set of key international norms – sovereign equality, non-interference and the right to development – that were interpreted in the latter part of the twentieth century to underpin a distinctly 'permissive' liberal order in which the average size of the state shrunk dramatically. This order, which the leaders of SIDS themselves helped to create, *permitted* tiny countries to exist *as* equal members of the international community despite the widespread fear that they could not be self-sufficient (according to mainstream economic conceptions) or self-reliant (according to the assumptions of mainstream international relations). 'Permissiveness' therefore refers to the fact that most SIDS do not maintain standing armies with which to defend themselves. Many are heavily indebted, rely on ODA for basic services, do not have their own national currency, and so on. Yet the international community affords a country such as Tuvalu, with a population of little more than 11,000 persons and some of the highest ODA per capita ratios in the world, the same vote in the UNGA as China or the US. If this order were a truly anarchic, self-help system in which states were merging like firms in a process of competitive selection, then Tuvalu and all the countries like it would not exist; they would either be plundered or ignored entirely.

Third, while all of this may appear obvious, restating it matters more today than ever precisely because we are potentially emerging from the interregnum into a new era. At present, the dominant concepts that explain SIDS development – encompassed in the so-called vulnerability and resilience debate – tend to overlook this crucial point. Instead, they focus on intervening variables in a bid to determine when and how inherent size-related constraints can be overcome by the benefits of size-related advantages. This is important work – it challenges the conventional assumptions of both mainstream economics and IR (Bishop 2012) – but it is only useful *if* we assume that the order *is* and *will remain* stable. Put differently: most thinking on SIDS, until now, has implicitly taken the existence of a permissive order for granted. This has the effect of naturalising it, when, in fact, it is historically and ideologically contingent, rooted in a particular time and place. Many have, of course, explicitly critiqued the malign effects of neoliberal globalisation, but this reinforces the point: the order itself is still seen as static, an overweening constraint on action or, in more optimistic accounts, something that enables it.

By contrast, we seek to problematise the *nature* and *character* of this order and cast it as a distinct era in human history underpinned by a particular constellation of norms that shape state preferences and social compromises (see Cox 1981). So, the main thread tying our argument together is the notion that the permissive liberal order itself is changing, and this, in turn, is both a cause and effect of the shifting balance of state power, the emergence and proliferation of new social forces, patterns of contestation between them, and dominant ideas, norms, and values. In fact, the permissive order is beset by three interlocking crises: (i) an economic crisis that is a function of the inherent contradictions of neoliberal globalisation but was brought to a head by the global financial crisis and further exacerbated by COVID-19 and its aftermath; (ii) a geopolitical crisis brought about by, in the first instance, the changing distribution of global power, the waning of US hegemony and increasing tension between, especially but not exclusively, the US and China; and (iii) the now rapidly accelerating climate crisis, which is long-running but is approaching a series of key tipping points that will intensify economic and geopolitical problems. In short, the combination of these three intersecting crises threatens the continuation of the system of norms and associated rules upon which SIDS developmental gains have been built.

At the same time, the nature of the order is up for grabs: liberalising tendencies co-exist with illiberalising ones, and the future of multilateral politics and globalising economics is very much an open question. So, we have sought to understand the possible effects of this change by way of a three-part heuristic. Scenario One sees the return of a more competitive, self-help system with some advantages for SIDS, including the ability to leverage increased attention from countries such as the US and China to their advantage. We think this scenario will ultimately be to their detriment as it will undermine all three of the key norms of the post–Second World War order. These norms have enabled them to generate unique service-based economies that have delivered levels of development that are the envy of many other postcolonial states. A return to a more competitive, self-help system would see these gains reversed and a return of forms of exploitation – of peoples, communities, and environments – common to the Age of Empire when the large conquered the small.

Scenario Two is the creation of a more muscular liberal order, which might be more popular among readers of this Element, but will present considerable dangers, too. The reason is that, while a more muscular liberal order would retain the right to development as a core pillar in its regime of rights, it would increasingly come to see the norms of sovereign equality and non-interference as a barrier to pursuing it. Instead, a more muscular liberalism would seek to create its version of a more cosmopolitan, individualist future by further shifting authority from the nation state to regional and international forms of governance. International systems that govern state behaviour would promote equality rather than equity, where SIDS, the weakest, are given the same benefits and opportunities as the strongest states, and are forced to play by the same rules. This would be to the detriment of SIDS whose unlikely statehood is premised on structured inequity that provides them with a disproportionate level of influence for populations of their size in regional and international regimes, especially when working together as a collective as they have done with such success in climate negotiations. Instead, their communities would have to rely on the benevolence and technical remedies of faraway policymakers in IOs to a far greater extent than at present, with even fewer levers to exert influence over them.

Scenario Three is the future we prefer. It involves augmenting the order that SIDS helped create and has underpinned their developmental gains over the last three decades by holding the norms that sustain it in productive tension. SIDS are the structurally weakest members of the international system by virtue of their size, whether measured by military, economy, or population. A permissive order provides them with the greatest degree of choice over their own affairs. All other things being equal, we place great stock in the idea of self-determination and the ability of communities to govern themselves. We believe that the relative developmental success many SIDS achieved in recent decades, tempered as it is by inequality, enduring colonial legacies and environmental degradation, support this view.

What Should Policymakers Do Now?

Based on our understanding of how SIDS have achieved important developmental gains over the last three decades and the threat that the immediate, interwoven crisis presents to them, we think policy makers should immediately seek to:

1. alter the way development assistance is allocated, as current formulations do not account for relatively wealthy yet highly vulnerable states;
2. generate new forms of debt relief that will arrest the current debt trap in SIDS, releasing funds that can be used to provide better public services and address social issues;
3. improve climate financing mechanisms, so that promised adaptation funds in particular are both easier to access and can be more easily absorbed to strengthen resilience of SIDS;

4. use international law to press for clarity on responsibilities and seek compensation for climate and environmental harms suffered by SIDS; and
5. reform the international financial institutions themselves, particularly the MDBs, ensuring SIDS' priorities are better represented in these changes.

These options are illustrative not exhaustive but we favour them because they give SIDS a chance to survive this critical juncture. There are other solutions we have argued for elsewhere (see Bishop et al. 2021), including migration schemes and those such as trust funds to which we are intuitively attracted but are yet to fully explore. The emphasis on these instruments is as much in the broad thrust as much as the specifics: they all seek to make the order more permissive of SIDS and alleviate their condition in such a way that enables them to create new, niche markets. By doing so they are able to maintain and even increase developmental gains made over recent decades. These options thus function as concrete examples of proposals that SIDS can and should push for, thereby substantiating our more abstract and historical account of the key factors that have underpinned their success and the critical juncture we all now face.

In the medium term, there is a much broader menu of options for reformers. For example, we favour:

1. expanding but democratising and constraining multilateral organisations. SIDS need representation in the G20, for example, with Singapore, an AOSIS member, a possible candidate and site of a permanent secretariat;
2. further reform of the development architecture to recognise the unique circumstances of SIDS and the accumulated historical debts of colonisers; and;
3. recasting how IOs support climate adaptation, to include but also go beyond loss and damage compensation, while also recommitting the world to more aggressive targets.

These proposals are more radical and, again, are only indicative. But the overall orientation towards enhanced permissiveness is the same.

Most significantly, if our explanation of the contemporary developmental experience in SIDS has purchase, then these types of policy changes will ultimately larger states, too, because a system that is permissive of small states will also sustain the international order as a whole. We are not saying that they will lead to dramatic shifts in levels of wealth and associated standards of living that might be imagined under more radical proposals for economic re-ordering like those outlined historically under the NIEO, for example. We are also certainly not saying that, in an ideal world, these would be either our preferred choices or the limit of our aspiration. But, we do not live in an ideal world. So, we acknowledge – and rebut below – that the future we lean towards might strike many as insufficiently ambitious. Crucially, though, we think it has the advantage of being possible to obtain. SIDS helped create the order that was advantageous to their development and that of others during the latter half of the twentieth century. It therefore stands to reason that they can help extend and improve it, too.

Anticipating Potential Criticisms

All theories, but especially those that involve gazing into the academic equivalent of a crystal ball, have their limitations. We briefly consider some of them as a way of fleshing out our argument but also buttressing it. The point is that, in making these claims, we have anticipated some of the most obvious criticisms. We are under no illusions that this will satisfy everyone that our narrative is persuasive. But we hope it does reassure readers that we have at least considered its limits.

Caricature

The first and most obvious potential criticism is that the three scenarios are caricatures. To some extent we agree, albeit we have used the fancier academic word – heuristic – to describe the fact that we are working with abstractions. The reason we think this is a viable method is hinted at in the opening paragraph of this section: we see ourselves as being in the business of sense-making not prediction. We do not know what the future will hold. We can imagine possible futures and the types of choices that would lead from here to there. But our narratives are unequivocally not facts for the fairly obvious reason that the future has not happened yet. They are 'rules of thumb' that we hope are nevertheless plausible if we take the standard of plausibility to be that our readers could imagine them occurring. We have also attempted to buttress the plausibility of our heuristic by considering the range of possible futures in each scenario. We are conscious that this will likely still not satisfy readers interested in empirical precision and fine-grained differentiation, either between countries, regions, or institutions. We are comfortable with that. This is not that type of Element. We have sought to paint on a larger canvass and this necessarily entails broad brushstrokes. We hope that in doing so we have provided insights that make the inherent trade-offs worth it. But that is for our readers to judge.

Conservatism

A much more pointed criticism that we have grappled throughout the writing process is that the scenario we favour – the augmentation or enhancement of a permissive liberal order – might strike many as an inherently conservative option, resting as it does on the continuation of colonially constituted capitalist modes of production and consumption, unequal globalisation, disregard for human rights, and forms of environmental exploitation that have led to untold suffering and injustice. From this perspective, what SIDS need instead is not augmentation or enhancement, but radical, through-going change of the type imagined at the beginning of the current order amidst decolonisation which was then watered down and eventually abandoned because it did not advantage larger states (Getachew 2019). In this case, the problem with our analysis is not, as earlier, that too much is left to the imagination, but rather we have not been anywhere near imaginative enough!

We have a lot of sympathy with this view. We also hope that in Section 3 in particular, where we discuss the effects the current order has had on SIDS societies, we have demonstrated that we are fully aware of the downsides of the – in many ways dysfunctional – capitalist economies it has created. The point is that we have not arrived at this position because we are naive or unaware. We could argue that what we propose is more clear-eyed and realistic about what is possible rather than what is desirable. To some extent we think that is true. But we also worry deeply about the logic of consequences contained in more radical proposals. In particular, we fear that advocates of more radical alternatives are typically prepared to jettison one or more of the three norms on which our explanation turns. For example, arguments for global socialism or eco-authoritarianism would also likely obliterate the norms of sovereign equality and non-interference, albeit in different ways to muscular liberalism. Both would leave SIDS and their communities vulnerable to the whims of universalist ideals and technocratic interventions. Similarly, a radical environmentalism that sought to return the world to a pre-modern relationship with nature would likely deny SIDS both climate justice *and* the developmental gains enjoyed by communities in other countries. We struggle to see how this is to their benefit. By the same token, we recognise the demand for radical reparatory justice demanded by increasing numbers of thinkers to repair the horrors of colonialism and slavery, and we endorse this agenda fully (see Beckles 2013, 2021). But this is not, of itself, a challenge to our argument in this Element, not least because the nature of this debate differs quite markedly across (and even within) SIDS regions given their varying colonial experiences. In fact, a reparatory agenda is entirely compatible with our argument here – even though it has not been a core focus of the discussion – and is arguably more likely to succeed within an enhanced permissive order than under either of the other two scenarios.

Ultimately, then, we believe that what we propose is preferable both because it is possible but also because it is the 'least bad' outcome. We acknowledge that this rests on a logic of negation. But we reject the charge that it is inherently conservative. Only half a century ago, amidst the global movement towards decolonisation, the idea that SIDS should be able to assert their sovereign equality, protect themself against foreign interference, and pursue their right to development, represented a radical re-ordering of international affairs. So, our argument is not against progress. Rather, all of the supposedly radical alternatives for further progress ironically end up looking more like the order that was left behind at independence than the one a previous generation of SIDS leaders helped create precisely because they thought it would improve their postcolonial condition. We think that, for the most part, they were right.

Agency

The key reason we agree with this first generation of SIDS leaders and think a permissive order is preferable, is that they sought to create a world that revolved around the principle of self-determination: they wanted SIDS to face a future of 'choices rather than imperatives' (Sharman 2017: 560). To be sure, they knew self-determination had to be balanced by the need to ensure viability, which is why we see SIDS simultaneously asserting their sovereignty and independence at the same time as they pursue development via forms of integration and sovereignty sales (Corbett 2023). But the point is they wanted to create a world in which *how* SIDS balanced that inherent dilemma was largely up to them. The founders of these states could not have imagined a future in which economic development would be dependent on sectors such as tourism or financial services given most were raised in a world in which sugar and other plantation crops were king. But they did envisage a scenario in which they had more control over their destiny than they did during the Age of Empire. Their successors then grasped the world they created to pursue niches and forms of enclave capitalism that generated substantial levels of growth (Baldacchino 2010), as we saw in Section 2. This entrepreneurialism implies agency. We therefore see our preference for Scenario Three as a vote of confidence in that agency rather than a concession to conservatism and structural inequality.

We anticipate two main criticisms of this argument. The first, as earlier, is that it is naive and the second that it is undeserved. By centring self-determination, we have made a judgement that, all other things being equal, SIDS are best placed to make decisions for themselves. By contrast, both realists and liberals would argue that this faith is quaint yet ultimately absurd. They would do so for different reasons: where the realists would say most choices, especially by leaders of small states, are irrelevant considering structural forces, liberals are more likely to say that our faith in them is misplaced as leaders are too fallible to be trusted with the future. At best their decision-making is susceptible to bias, both conscious and unconscious. At worst they are self-serving and corrupt. Either way, the main purpose of a liberal 'rules based' order is to reduce their discretion and by implication the impact of their decisions on outcomes.

We do not deny that leaders can be biased and self-interested. That would be a fruitless claim to make given the surfeit of empirical examples. Rather, our counter argument turns on two claims: (1) that a 'rules-based' order still has rulers who interpret and enforce; and (2) that these rulers, who might be politicians from larger states, international civil servants, judges, and so on, are just as likely to be as biased and self-interested as SIDS politicians. In which case, faced with a choice between 'tyranny' from abroad and 'tyranny' at home, we think the latter – which is nested in, but not dominated by international institutions and regimes – is more likely to make decisions that have the best chance of benefitting communities over the longue durée. This preference for self-determination is the same logic that drove the end of empire. Of course, nobody championed decolonisation on the basis that it would empower local tyrants – indeed, many opposed it on those grounds – but we venture that, even despite disappointment at what self-government has achieved, and the relative economic success of small non-sovereign island jurisdictions, it has nearly always proven much better for SIDS than direct rule from afar. We see no reason why the future would be any different.

Hypocrisy

The final, most obvious but also most pointed criticism of an Element that advocates for the augmentation of a permissive liberal order on the grounds that it values self-determination and the choices of leaders, is that our acceptance of 'least bad' local 'tyranny' might make sense when you view SIDS from abroad, living comfortably in the Global North. But it is a hollow argument if you live on a small island and experience all of the problems of the order first hand. We have considerable sympathy with this point, in part because the majority of the authorship either hails from or has lived in a SIDS country for a period, too. For this reason, we do not deny the problems with the current order anymore more than we have sought to highlight the flaws in alternatives. Rather, the main purpose of the Element is to keep what is good and which contributed to gains made over recent decades and find ways to improve the SIDS condition by proposing amendments. Whether we succeed is out of our control. But if this Element and the thinking behind it have any positive impact it will be because of the hypocrisy – our privileged view from afar will have enabled us to see patterns clearly and communicate them to those who can make a difference – not despite it.

A World *for* SIDS

The main difference we seek to make is to advocate for a world order that values a diversity of governing forms. This is the essence of the SIDS agenda: they are different because of the characteristics that make them SIDS and because they are different they need a special deal or bargain. By implication, off-the-shelf one-size-fits-all solutions will not work for everyone. This claim has become widely if not completely accepted among international diplomats and civil servants. But it is also under pressure because of the crisis of economy, geopolitics, and climate we all face. In extreme circumstances, everyone is more likely to reach for extreme responses. These typically prioritise consequentialist logics: that the ends justify the means. In such times, there is a tendency to view diversity and special and differential treatment as a weakness that diverts attention from the 'real' problems. Our hope is that, by highlighting the ways diversity is protected by permissiveness, and the benefits it has brought, both to SIDS and the broader international system, we can show that it is both a worthy means and end. A world created *for* SIDS is likely a better world for all states, too.

References

Abbott, Kenneth W. 2017. 'Orchestrating Experimentation in Non-state Environmental Commitments'. *Environmental Politics* 26 (4): 738–63. https://doi.org/10.1080/09644016.2017.1319631.

Acharya, Amitav. 2014. *The End of American World Order*. Cambridge: Polity.

——— 2017. 'After Liberal Hegemony: The Advent of a Multiplex World Order'. *Ethics & International Affairs* 31 (3): 271–85. https://doi.org/10.1017/S089267941700020X.

——— 2018. *Constructing Global Order: Agency and Change in World Politics*. Cambridge: Cambridge University Press. https://doi.org/10.1017/9781316756768.

Agius, Karl, Francesco Sindico, Giulia Sajeva, and Godfrey Baldacchino. 2022. '"Splendid Isolation": Embracing Islandness in a Global Pandemic'. *Island Studies Journal* 17 (1): 44–65. https://doi.org/10.24043/isj.163.

Alami, Ilias, and Adam D. Dixon . 2024. *The Spectre of State Capitalism*. Critical Frontiers of Theory, Research, and Policy in International Development Studies. Oxford: Oxford University Press.

Almeida, Paul. 2019. 'Climate Justice and Sustained Transnational Mobilization'. *Globalizations* 16 (7): 973–79. https://doi.org/10.1080/14747731.2019.1651518.

Almela, Victoria Dominguez, Kwasi Appeaning Addo, Jack Corbett, et al. 2023. 'Science and Policy Lessons Learned from a Decade of Adaptation to the Emergent Risk of Sargassum Proliferation across the Tropical Atlantic'. *Environmental Research Communications* 5 (6): 061002. https://doi.org/10.1088/2515-7620/acd493.

Arellano-Verdejo, Javier, Hugo E. Lazcano-Hernandez, and Nancy Cabanillas-Terán. 2019. 'ERISNet: Deep Neural Network for Sargassum Detection along the Coastline of the Mexican Caribbean'. *PeerJ* 7 (May): e6842. https://doi.org/10.7717/peerj.6842.

Ashe, John W., Robert Van Lierop, and Anilla Cherian. 1999. 'The Role of the Alliance of Small Island States (AOSIS) in the Negotiation of the United Nations Framework Convention on Climate Change (UNFCCC)'. *Natural Resources Forum* 23 (3): 209–20. https://doi.org/10.1111/j.1477-8947.1999.tb00910.x.

Baccaro, Lucio, Mark Blyth, and Jonas Pontusson. 2022. *Diminishing Returns: The New Politics of Growth and Stagnation*. Oxford: Oxford University Press.

Baker, Andrew. 2018a. 'Macroprudential Regimes and the Politics of Social Purpose'. *Review of International Political Economy* 25 (3): 293–316. https://doi.org/10.1080/09692290.2018.1459780.

2018b. 'Macroprudential Regimes and the Politics of Social Purpose'. *Review of International Political Economy* 25 (3): 293–316. https://doi .org/10.1080/09692290.2018.1459780.

Baker, Kerryn. 2018. 'Great Expectations: Gender and Political Representation in the Pacific Islands'. *Government and Opposition* 53 (3): 542–68. https:// doi.org/10.1017/gov.2016.54.

Baldacchino, Godfrey. 1993. 'Bursting the Bubble: The Pseudo-development Strategies of Microstates'. *Development and Change* 24 (1): 29–52. https://doi.org/10.1111/j.1467-7660.1993.tb00476.x.

2010. *Island Enclaves: Offshoring Strategies, Creative Governance, and Subnational Island Jurisdictions*. Montreal: McGill-Queen's University Press. www.jstor.org/stable/j.ctt7zq30.

2020. 'How Far Can One Go?: How Distance Matters in Island Development'. www.um.edu.mt/library/oar/handle/123456789/56318.

ed. 2023. *The Success of Small States in International Relations: Mice that Roar?* 1st ed. New York: Routledge.

Baldacchino, Godfrey, and David Milne. 2009. *The Case for Non-sovereignty: Lessons from Sub-national Island Jurisdictions*. London: Routledge.

Baldacchino, Godfrey, and Geoffrey Bertram. 2009. 'The Beak of the Finch: Insights into the Economic Development of Small Economies'. *The Round Table* 98 (401): 141–60. https://doi.org/10.1080/00358530902757867.

Ban, Cornel. 2016. *Ruling Ideas: How Global Neoliberalism Goes Local*. New York: Oxford University Press.

Banivanua Mar, Tracey. 2016. *Decolonisation and the Pacific: Indigenous Globalisation and the Ends of Empire*. Critical Perspectives on Empire. Cambridge: Cambridge University Press. https://doi.org/10.1017/CBO9781139794688.

Barclay, Jenni, Emily Wilkinson, Carole S. White, et al. 2019. 'Historical Trajectories of Disaster Risk in Dominica'. *International Journal of Disaster Risk Science* 10 (2): 149–65. https://doi.org/10.1007/s13753-019-0215-z.

Barnett, Jon. 2003. "Security and Climate Change." *Global Environmental Change* 13 (1): 7–17. https://doi.org/10.1016/S0959-3780(02)00080-8.

Barriteau, Eudine. 1998. 'Theorizing Gender Systems and the Project of Modernity in the Twentieth-Century Caribbean'. *Feminist Review* 59 (1): 186–210. https://doi.org/10.1080/014177898339523.

Barrow, Christine. 1998. 'Caribbean Masculinity and Family: Revisiting "Marginality" and "Reputation"'. In *Caribbean Portraits: Essays on Gender Ideologies and Identities*, edited by Christine Barrow, 339–58. Kingston: Ian Randle.

Beckles, Hilary McD. 2013. *Britain's Black Debt: Reparations for Caribbean Slavery and Native Genocide*. Mona, Jamaica: University of the West Indies Press.

Beckles, Hilary. 2021. *How Britain Underdeveloped the Caribbean*. Mona, Jamaica: UWI Press.

Bell, Duncan. 2015. *Remaking the World: Essays on Liberalism and Empire*. 1st ed. Princeton, NJ: Princeton University Press.

Benwell, Richard. 2011. 'The Canaries in the Coalmine: Small States as Climate Change Champions'. *The Round Table* 100 (413): 199–211. https://doi.org/10.1080/00358533.2011.565632.

Bernstein, Steven. 2002. 'Liberal Environmentalism and Global Environmental Governance'. *Global Environmental Politics* 2 (3): 1–16. https://doi.org/10.1162/152638002320310509.

Betzold, Carola. 2010. '"Borrowing" Power to Influence International Negotiations: AOSIS in the Climate Change Regime, 1990–1997'. *Politics* 30 (3): 131–48. https://doi.org/10.1111/j.1467-9256.2010.01377.x.

Bevir, Mark, Oliver Daddow, and Ian Hall. 2013. 'Introduction: Interpreting British Foreign Policy'. *The British Journal of Politics and International Relations* 15 (2): 163–74. https://doi.org/10.1111/j.1467-856X.2012.00537.x.

Biermann, Frank, Jeroen Oomen, Aarti Gupta, et al. 2022. 'Solar Geoengineering: The Case for an International Non-use Agreement'. *WIREs Climate Change* 13 (3): e754. https://doi.org/10.1002/wcc.754.

Biermann, Frank, Michele M. Betsill, Joyeeta Gupta, et al. 2010. 'Earth System Governance: A Research Framework'. *International Environmental Agreements: Politics, Law and Economics* 10 (4): 277–98. https://doi.org/10.1007/s10784-010-9137-3.

Biermann, Frank, and Philipp Pattberg. 2008. 'Global Environmental Governance: Taking Stock, Moving Forward'. *Annual Review of Environment and Resources* 33 (1): 277–94. https://doi.org/10.1146/annurev.environ.33.050707.085733.

Biermann, Frank, Philipp Pattberg, Harro van Asselt, and Fariborz Zelli. 2009. 'The Fragmentation of Global Governance Architectures: A Framework for Analysis'. *Global Environmental Politics* 9 (4): 14–40. https://direct.mit.edu/glep/article-abstract/9/4/14/14757/The-Fragmentation-of-Global-Governance.

Bishop, Matthew Louis. 2010. 'Tourism as a Small-State Development Strategy: Pier Pressure in the Eastern Caribbean?' *Progress in Development Studies* 10 (2): 99–114. https://doi.org/10.1177/146499340901000201.

———. 2011. 'Slaying the "Westmonster" in the Caribbean? Constitutional Reform in St Vincent and the Grenadines'. *The British Journal of Politics and International Relations* 13 (3): 420–37. https://doi.org/10.1111/j.1467-856X.2010.00432.x.

———. 2012. 'The Political Economy of Small States: Enduring Vulnerability?' *Review of International Political Economy* 19 (5): 942–60. https://www.tandfonline.com/doi/abs/10.1080/09692290.2011.635118.

———. 2013. *The Political Economy of Caribbean Development*. 2013th ed. Basingstoke: Palgrave Macmillan.

———. 2015. 'Caribbean Development in the Midst of New Regional and Global Dynamics'. *Forum on the Future of the Caribbean*, hosted by the Ministry of Foreign Affairs of Trinidad and Tobago, the United Nations Development Programme (UNDP) and the University of the West Indies, Port of Spain, Trinidad, 6th–8th May 2015.

———. 2016. 'Rethinking the Political Economic of Development Beyond "The Rise of the BRICS"'. SPERI Paper. Sheffield Political Economy Research Institute.

———. 2018. 'China Crisis?' In *The Coming Crisis (Building a Sustainable Political Economy: SPERI Research Policy)*, edited by Colin Hay and Tom Hunt. Building a Sustainable Political Economy: SPERI Research and Policy, 103–11. United Kingdom: Palgrave Macmillan.

———. 20 October 2022. 'The BRICS Countries: Where Next and What Impact on the Global Economy?' *Economics Observatory* (blog). www.economicsobservatory.com/the-brics-countries-where-next-and-what-impact-on-the-global-economy.

Bishop, Matthew Louis, and Andrew F. Cooper. 2018. 'The FIFA Scandal and the Distorted Influence of Small States'. *Global Governance* 24 (1): 21–40.

Bishop, Matthew Louis, and Anthony Payne. 2010. 'Caribbean Regional Governance and the Sovereignty/Statehood Problem'. The Centre for International Governance Innovation (CIGI) Caribbean Paper No. 8. www.cigionline.org/static/documents/caribbean_paper_8_0.

Bishop, Matthew Louis, and Anthony Payne. 2021a. 'The Political Economies of Different Globalizations: Theorizing Reglobalization'. *Globalizations* 18 (1): 1–21. https://doi.org/10.1080/14747731.2020.1779963.

Bishop, Matthew Louis, and Anthony Payne. 2021b. 'Steering towards Reglobalization: Can a Reformed G20 Rise to the Occasion?' *Globalizations* 18 (1): 120–40. https://doi.org/10.1080/14747731.2020.1779964.

Bishop, Matthew Louis, and Dylan Kerrigan. 2023. 'Policing Drugs in the Caribbean'. In *Drug Law Enforcement, Policing and Harm Reduction*, edited by Matthew Bacon and Jack Spicer, 132–50. London: Routledge.

Bishop, Matthew Louis, and Courtney Lindsay. 2024. *Breaking the Cycle of Debt in SIDS: the Jamaica Experience*. London: ODI. https://media.odi .org/documents/Jamaica_case_study.pdf.

Bishop, Matthew Louis. 2018. 'Developing Democracy, Democratizing Development: A Backlash against Hegemonic Norms and Practice?' In *Handbook on Development and Social Change*, edited by G. Conor Fagan, and Ronaldo Munck, 173–89. Cheltenham: Edward Elgar. www.elgaron line.com/edcollchap/edcoll/9781786431547/9781786431547.00017.xml.

Bishop, Matthew Louis, George Carter, Courtney Lindsay, Henrique Lopes-Valença, and Emily Wilkinson. 2023. 'A Global Bargain for Resilient Prosperity in Small Island Developing States: Priorities for the Antigua and Barbuda Accord for SIDS (2024–2034)'. Policy Brief. London: ODI. https:// odi.org/en/publications/a-global-bargain-for-resilient-prosperity-in-sids/.

Bishop, Matthew Louis, Jack Corbett, and Wouter Veenendaal. 2020. 'Labor Movements and Party System Development: Why Does the Caribbean Have Stable Two-Party Systems, but the Pacific Does Not?' *World Development* 126 (February): 104719. https://doi.org/10.1016/j.worlddev.2019.104719.

Bishop, Matthew Louis, Jessica Byron-Reid, Jack Corbett, and Wouter Veenendaal. 2022. 'Secession, Territorial Integrity and (Non)-sovereignty: Why Do Some Separatist Movements in the Caribbean Succeed and Others Fail?' *Ethnopolitics* 21 (5): 538–60. https://doi.org/10.1080/17449057.2021 .1975414.

Bishop, Matthew Louis, Michelle Scobie, Jack Corbett, et al. 2021a. 'Towards Sustained Development in Small Island Developing States: Why We Need to Reshape Global Governance'. Working Paper. London: ODI. https://odi .org/en/publications/towards-sustained-development-in-small-island-developing-states-why-we-need-to-reshape-global-governance/.

Bishop, Matthew Louis, and Peg Murray-Evans. 2020. 'Five Little B(R)ICS: Huffing and Puffing, but Not Blowing Your House In'. *New Political Economy* 25 (5): 691–702. https://doi.org/10.1080/13563467.2019.1584166.

Bishop, Matthew Louis, Tony Heron, and Anthony Payne. 2013a. 'Caribbean Development Alternatives and the CARIFORUM-European Union Economic Partnership Agreement'. *Journal of International Relations and Development* 16 (1): 82–110. https://doi.org/10.1057/jird.2012.5.

2013b. 'Caribbean Development Alternatives and the CARIFORUM – European Union Economic Partnership Agreement'. *Journal of International*

Relations and Development 16 (1): 82–110. https://doi.org/10.1057/jird.2012.5.

Bishop, Matthew Louis, and Zhang Xiaotong. 2020. 'Why Is China a Reluctant Leader of the World Trade Organization?' *New Political Economy* 25 (5): 755–72. https://doi.org/10.1080/13563467.2019.1584170.

Brereton, Bridget. 1981. *A History of Modern Trinidad, 1783–1962*. Kingston: Heinemann.

Briguglio, Lino, Gordon Cordina, Nadia Farrugia, and Stephanie Vella. 2009. 'Economic Vulnerability and Resilience: Concepts and Measurements'. *Oxford Development Studies* 37 (3): 229–47. https://doi.org/10.1080/13600810903089893.

Browning, Christopher S. 2006. 'Small, Smart and Salient? Rethinking Identity in the Small States Literature'. *Cambridge Review of International Affairs* 19 (4): 669–84. https://doi.org/10.1080/09557570601003536.

Burch, Sarah, Heike Schroeder, Steve Rayner, and Jennifer Wilson. 2013. 'Novel Multisector Networks and Entrepreneurship: The Role of Small Businesses in the Multilevel Governance of Climate Change'. *Environment and Planning C: Government and Policy* 31 (5): 822–40. https://doi.org/10.1068/c1206.

Buzdugan, Stephen, and Anthony Payne. 2016. *The Long Battle for Global Governance*. 1st ed. London: Routledge.

Capoccia, Giovanni, and R. Daniel Kelemen. 2007. 'The Study of Critical Junctures: Theory, Narrative, and Counterfactuals in Historical Institutionalism'. *World Politics* 59 (3): 341–69. https://www.cambridge.org/core/journals/world-polit ics/article/study-of-critical-junctures-theory-narrative-and-counterfactuals-in-historical-institutionalism/BAAE0860F1F641357C29C9AC72A54758.

Cardoso, Fernando Henrique, Enzo Faletto, and Marjory Mattingly Urquidi. 1979. *Dependency and Development in Latin America*. Berkeley: University of California Press.

Cavanough, Edward Acton. 2024. *Divided Isles: Solomon Islands and the China Switch*. Melbourne: Latrobe University Press.

Chan, Nicholas. 2018. '"Large Ocean States": Sovereignty, Small Islands, and Marine Protected Areas in Global Oceans Governance'. *Global Governance* 24 (4): 537–55. https://brill.com/view/journals/gg/24/4/article-p537_5.xml.

Chan, Sander, Idil Boran, Harro van Asselt, Gabriela Iacobuta, et al. 2019. 'Promises and Risks of Nonstate Action in Climate and Sustainability Governance'. *WIREs Climate Change* 10 (3): e572. https://doi.org/10.1002/wcc.572

Chan, Sander, Idil Boran, Harro van Asselt, Paula Ellinger, et al. 2021. 'Climate Ambition and Sustainable Development for a New Decade: A Catalytic

Framework'. *Global Policy* 12 (3): 245–59. https://doi.org/10.1111/1758-5899.12932.

Clegg, Peter. 2002. *The Caribbean Banana Trade: From Colonialism to Globalization*. 2002nd ed. Baskingstoke: Palgrave Macmillan.

Climate Finance Access Network. 2023. 'Accessing Climate Finance: Challenges and Opportunities for Small Island Developing States'. United Nations. https://www.un.org/ohrlls/sites/www.un.org.ohrlls/files/accessing_climate_finance_challenges_sids_report.pdf.

Cockayne, James. 2016. *Hidden Power: The Strategic Logic of Organized Crime*. 1st ed. New York: Oxford University Press.

Cockayne, James, and Summer Walker. 2015. 'What Comes after the War on Drugs – Flexibility, Fragmentation or Principled Pluralism?' Policy Report. New York: United Nations University. https://idpc.net/publica tions/2015/11/unu-report-launch-what-comes-after-the-war-on-drugs.

Cole, Rodney V., ed. 1993. *Pacific 2010: Challenging the Future*, edited by Rodney V Cole. Canberra: National Centre for Development Studies, Research School of Pacific Studies, Australian National University.

Connell, John. 2013. *Islands at Risk?: Environments, Economies and Contemporary Change*. Cheltenham; Northampton, MA: Edward Elgar.

——— 2022. 'COVID-19 in the Pacific Territories: Isolation, Borders and the Complexities of Governance'. *Asia & the Pacific Policy Studies* 9 (3): 394–407. https://doi.org/10.1002/app5.364.

Connell, John, and Jack Corbett. 2016. 'Deterritorialisation: Reconceptualising Development in the Pacific Islands'. *Global Society* 30 (4): 583–604. https://doi.org/10.1080/13600826.2016.1158701.

Cooley, Alexander, and Daniel Nexon. 2020. *Exit from Hegemony: The Unraveling of the American Global Order*. New York: Oxford University Press.

Corbett, Jack. 2020. 'Territory, Islandness, and the Secessionist Imaginary: Why Do Very Small Communities Favour Autonomy over Integration?' *Nations and Nationalism* 26 (4): 1087–1103. https://doi.org/10.1111/nana.12597.

——— 2023. *Statehood À La Carte in the Caribbean and the Pacific: Secession, Regionalism, and Postcolonial Politics*. Oxford: Oxford University Press.

Corbett, Jack, and Wouter Veenendaal. 2018. 'Persisting against All Odds'. In *Democracy in Small States: Persisting against All Odds*, edited by Jack Corbett and Wouter Veenendaal. Oxford: Oxford University Press. https://doi.org/10.1093/oso/9780198796718.003.0008.

Corbett, Jack, Xu Yi-chong, and Patrick Weller. 2021. *International Organizations and Small States: Participation, Legitimacy and Vulnerability*. Bristol: Bristol University Press.

Corbett, Jack, Yi-chong Xu, and Patrick Weller. 2019. 'Norm Entrepreneurship and Diffusion "from Below" in International Organisations: How the Competent Performance of Vulnerability Generates Benefits for Small States'. *Review of International Studies* 45 (4): 647–68. https://doi.org/10.1017/S0260210519000068.

Cox, Robert W. 1981. 'Social Forces, States and World Orders: Beyond International Relations Theory'. *Millennium* 10 (2): 126–55.

Crocombe, Ron. 2008. *The South Pacific*. 7th ed. Suva, Fi: IPS, University of the South Pacific.

Dellas, Eleni, Philipp Pattberg, and Michele Betsill. 2011. 'Agency in Earth System Governance: Refining a Research Agenda'. *International Environmental Agreements: Politics, Law and Economics* 11 (1): 85–98. https://doi.org/10.1007/s10784-011-9147-9.

Demas, William G. 1965. The Economics of Development in Small Countries: With Special Reference to the *Caribbean*. Montreal: McGill-Queen's Press-MQUP.

Demas, William G., Hilary Beckles, and Compton Bourne. 2009. *The Economics of Development in Small Countries: With Special Reference to the Caribbean*. Mona, Jamaica: University Press of the West Indies.

Dornan, Matthew, and Kalim U. Shah. 'Energy Policy, Aid, and the Development of Renewable Energy Resources in Small Island Developing States'. *Energy Policy* 98 (2016): 759–767. https://www.sciencedirect.com/science/article/pii/S030142151630266X.

Dornan, Matthew, and Jonathan Pryke. 2017. 'Foreign Aid to the Pacific: Trends and Developments in the Twenty-First Century'. *Asia & the Pacific Policy Studies* 4 (3): 386–404. https://doi.org/10.1002/app5.185.

Doumenge, Francois. 1989. *Basic Criteria for Estimating the Viability of Small Island States*. Utrecht, Netherlands: Eburon. www.um.edu.mt/library/oar/handle/123456789/77044.

Dreher, Tanja, and Michelle Voyer. 'Climate Refugees or Migrants? Contesting Media Frames on Climate Change Justice in the Pacific'. (2015): 58

Duncan, Ronald. 2008. 'Cultural and Economic Tensions in Pacific Islands' Futures', edited by Paresh Kumar Narayan. *International Journal of Social Economics* 35 (12): 919–29. https://doi.org/10.1108/03068290810911462.

——— 2018. 'Land Reform in Papua New Guinea: Securing Individual Title to Customary Owned Land'. *Policy* 34 (1), 15–20. https://openresearch-repository.anu.edu.au/handle/1885/264175.

Duvat, Virginie, Alexandre Magnan, and Frédéric Pouget. 2013. 'Exposure of Atoll Population to Coastal Erosion and Flooding: A South Tarawa Assessment, Kiribati'. *Sustainability Science* 8 (3): 423–40. https://doi .org/10.1007/s11625-013-0215-7.

Feeny, David, Fikret Berkes, Bonnie J. McCay, and James M. Acheson. 1990. 'The Tragedy of the Commons: Twenty-Two Years Later'. *Human Ecology* 18 (1): 1–19. https://doi.org/10.1007/BF00889070.

Feldman, Jonathan Michael. 2021. 'From the "Greta Thunberg Effect" to Green Conversion of Universities: The Reconstructive Praxis of Discursive Mobilizations'. *Discourse and Communication for Sustainable Education* 12 (1): 121–39. https://doi.org/10.2478/dcse-2021-0009.

Finnemore, Martha, and Kathryn Sikkink. 1998. 'International Norm Dynamics and Political Change'. *International Organization* 52 (4): 887–917. https:// doi.org/10.2307/j.ctt6wqpnp.

Firth, Stewart. 'Colonial Administration and the Invention of the Native'. In *The Cambridge history of the Pacific islanders*, edited by Donald Denoon, ed. p. 254. Cambridge: Cambridge University Press, 1997.

Firth, Stewart. 2000. 'Decolonization'. In *Remembrance of Pacific Pasts: An Invitation to Remake History*, edited by Robert Borofsky, 314–32. Canberra: University of Hawaii Press.

Fisk, Ernest Kelvin 1970. *The Political Economy of Independent Fiji*. Canberra: Australian National University Press.

Fradera, Josep M., and Christopher Schmidt-Nowara, eds. 2015. *Slavery and Antislavery in Spain's Atlantic Empire*. 1st ed. New York: Berghahn Books.

Frank, Andre Gunder. 1967. *Capitalism and Underdevelopment in Latin America*. Vol. 93. New York: NYU Press.

Fraser, Nancy. 2022. *Cannibal Capitalism: How Our System Is Devouring Democracy, Care, and the Planet – and What We Can Do About It*. 1st ed. New York: Verso.

Gascoigne, Joseph. 2023. 'Allowing Corruption and Dodging Accountability: The Negative Consequences of the Westminster System and Partisan Media in Small Caribbean States'. *New West Indian Guide / Nieuwe West-Indische Gids* 97 (3–4): 289–316. https://doi.org/10.1163/22134360-bja10025.

Gehring, Thomas, and Sebastian Oberthür. 2008. 'Interplay: Exploring Institutional Interaction'. In *Institutions and Environmental Change: Principal Findings, Applications, and Research Frontiers*, edited by Oran R. Young, Leslie A. King, and Heike Schroeder, 187–223.

Cambridge, MA: The MIT Press. https://doi.org/10.7551/mitpress/ 9780262240574.003.0006.

Getachew, Adom. 2019. *Worldmaking after Empire – The Rise and Fall of Self-Determination*. Princeton, NJ: Princeton University Press.

Girvan, Norman. 2010. 'Technification, Sweetification, Treatyfication: Politics of the Caribbean-EU Economic Partnership Agreement'. *Interventions* 12 (1): 100–111. https://doi.org/10.1080/13698010903553377.

Goldsmith, Michael. 2005. 'Theories of Governance and Pacific Microstates: The Cautionary Tale of Tuvalu'. *Asia Pacific Viewpoint* 46 (2): 105–14. https://doi.org/10.1111/j.1467-8373.2005.00270.x.

Government of Dominica. 2022. *Voluntary National Review of Dominica* Government of Dominica. https://hlpf.un.org/sites/default/files/vnrs/ 2022/VNR%202022%20Dominica%20Report.pdf.

Grainger, Alan. 2017. 'The Prospect of Global Environmental Relativities after an Anthropocene Tipping Point'. *Forest Policy and Economics* 79 (June): 36–49.

Green, Jessica F., and Graeme Auld. 2017. 'Unbundling the Regime Complex: The Effects of Private Authority'. *Transnational Environmental Law* 6 (2): 259–84. https://doi.org/10.1017/S2047102516000121, https://www.cambridge.org/ core/journals/transnational-environmental-law/article/unbundling-the-regime-complex-effects-of-private-authority/C64AED9E3020D8824DA42E C71A5AD01E.

Greenfield, Sidney M. 1977. 'Madeira and the Beginnings of New World Sugar Cane Cultivation and Plantation Slavery: A Study in Institution Building'. *Annals of the New York Academy of Sciences* 292 (1): 536–52. https://doi .org/10.1111/j.1749-6632.1977.tb47771.x.

Griffith, Ivelaw Lloyd. 1997. *Drugs and Security in the Caribbean: Sovereignty under Siege*. Illustrated ed. University Park, PA: State University Press.

Grøn, Caroline Howard, and Anders Wivel. 2011. 'Maximizing Influence in the European Union after the Lisbon Treaty: From Small State Policy to Smart State Strategy'. *Journal of European Integration* 33 (5): 523–39. https:// doi.org/10.1080/07036337.2010.546846.

Grydehøj, Adam, and Ilan Kelman. 2016. 'Island Smart Eco-Cities: Innovation, Secessionary Enclaves, and the Selling of Sustainability'. *Urban Island Studies* 2: 1–24. https://islandstudiesjournal.org/article/84778.

Grydehøj, Adam, and Ilan Kelman. 2017. 'The Eco-Island Trap: Climate Change Mitigation and Conspicuous Sustainability'. *Area* 49 (1): 106–13. https://doi.org/10.1111/area.12300.

Grynberg, Roman, ed. 2006. *WTO at the Margins: Small States and the Multilateral Trading System*. Illustrated ed. Cambridge: Cambridge University Press.

Guerra, Flávia. 2018. 'Mapping Offshore Renewable Energy Governance'. *Marine Policy* 89 (February): 21–33. https://doi.org/10.1016/j.marpol.2017.12.006.

Hardin, Garrett. 1968. 'The Tragedy of the Commons'. *Science* 162 (3859): 1243–48.

Hay, Colin. 2002. *Political Analysis: A Critical Introduction: 16*. 1st ed. Basingstoke: Palgrave Macmillan.

Held, David. 2010. *Cosmopolitanism: Ideals and Realities*. 1st ed. Cambridge: Polity.

Helleiner, Eric. 2010. 'A Bretton Woods Moment? The 2007–2008 Crisis and the Future of Global Finance'. *International Affairs (Royal Institute of International Affairs 1944-)* 86 (3): 619–36. http://www.jstor.org/stable/40664271.

Heron, Tony. 2008. 'Small States and the Politics of Multilateral Trade Liberalization'. *The Round Table* 97 (395): 243–57. https://doi.org/10.1080/00358530801962063.

——— 2011. 'Asymmetric Bargaining and Development Trade-Offs in the CARIFORUM-European Union Economic Partnership Agreement'. *Review of International Political Economy* 18 (3): 328–57. https://doi.org/10.1080/09692290.2010.481916.

——— 2013. *Pathways from Preferential Trade: The Politics of Trade Adjustment in Africa, the Caribbean and Pacific*. 2013th ed. Basingstoke: Palgrave Macmillan.

Hopewell, Kristen. 2019. 'US-China Conflict in Global Trade Governance: The New Politics of Agricultural Subsidies at the WTO'. *Review of International Political Economy* 26 (2): 207–31. https://doi.org/10.1080/09692290.2018.1560352.

——— 2020. *Clash of Powers: US-China Rivalry in Global Trade Governance*. Cambridge, United Kingdom ; New York: Cambridge University Press.

——— 2021. 'When the Hegemon Goes Rogue: Leadership Amid the US Assault on the Liberal Trading Order'. *International Affairs* 97 (4): 1025–43. https://doi.org/10.1093/ia/iiab073.

Hopkin, Jonathan. 2020. *Anti-system Politics: The Crisis of Market Liberalism in Rich Democracies*. Oxford: Oxford University Press.

Hosein, Roger. 2021. *Oil and Gas in Trinidad and Tobago: Managing the Resource Curse in a Small Petroleum-Exporting Economy*. 1st ed. New York: Palgrave Macmillan.

Hout, Wil. 2012. 'The Anti-politics of Development: Donor Agencies and the Political Economy of Governance'. *Third World Quarterly* 33 (3): 405–22. https://www.jstor.org/stable/41507178.

Hurley, G., Panwar, V., Wilkinson, E., Lindsay, C., Bishop, M, L. and E. 2024. *Mami Breaking the Cycle of Debt in Small Island Developing States*. London: ODI. https://media.odi.org/documents/ODI_SIDS_Breaking_the_cycle_of_debt_main_paper.pdf.

Ikenberry, G. John. 2008. 'The Rise of China and the Future of the West: Can the Liberal System Survive?' *Foreign Affairs* 87 (1): 23–37. https://www.jstor.org/stable/20020265.

2020. 'The Next Liberal Order'. *Foreign Affairs*, 9 June 2020. www.foreignaffairs.com/articles/united-states/2020-06-09/next-liberal-order.

Ingebritsen, Christine, Iver Neumann, and Sieglinde Gstöhl, eds. 2012. *Small States in International Relations*. Seattle: University of Washington.

Insanally, Rudy. 2012. *Multilateral Diplomacy for Small States: 'The Art of Letting Others Have Your Way'*. 1st ed. Georgetown, Guyana: Guyenterprise Advertising Agency.

International Labour Organization. 2020. 'Women in the World of Work: Pending Challenges for Achieving Effective Equality in Latin America and the Caribbean (Thematic Labour Overview, 5)'. Lima: ILO / Regional Officefor Latin America and the Caribbean. https://www.ilo.org/media/401956/download.

International Renewable Energy Agency. 2023. 'SIDS Lighthouses Initiative: Progress and Way Forward'. Abu Dhabi: International Renewable Energy Agency.

IPBES. 2022. 'Global Assessment Report on Biodiversity and Ecosystem Services of the Intergovernmental Science-Policy Platform on Biodiversity and Ecosystem Services'. Zenodo. Bonn, Germany: IPBES secretariat, https://doi.org/10.5281/zenodo.6417333.

IPBES. 2019. Weltbiodiversitätsrat. 'Intergovernmental Science-Policy Platform on Biodiversity and Ecosystem Services'. Summary for Policy Makers of the Global Assessment Report on Biodiversity and Ecosystem Services of the Intergovernmental Science-Policy Platform on Biodiversity and Ecosystem Services. Bonn, Germany: IPBES Secretariat.

Jackson, Guy, Alicia N'Guetta, Salvatore Paolo De Rosa, et al. 2023. 'An Emerging Governmentality of Climate Change Loss and Damage'. *Progress in Environmental Geography* 2 (1–2): 33–57. https://doi.org/10.1177/27539687221148748.

Jackson, Sarita. 2012. 'Small States and Compliance Bargaining in the WTO: An Analysis of the Antigua – US Gambling Services Case'. *Cambridge*

Review of International Affairs 25 (3): 367–85. https://doi.org/10.1080/ 09557571.2012.710588.

James, C. L. R. 2001. *The Black Jacobins: Toussaint L'Ouverture and the San Domingo Revolution.* Edited by James Walvin. New York: Penguin.

Jaschik, Kevin. 2014. 'Small States and International Politics: Climate Change, the Maldives and Tuvalu'. *International Politics* 51 (2): 272–93. https:// doi.org/10.1057/ip.2014.5.

John, Samuel, Elissaios Papyrakis, and Luca Tasciotti. 2020. 'Is There a Resource Curse in Timor-Leste? A Critical Review of Recent Evidence'. *Development Studies Research* 7 (1): 141–52. https://doi.org/10.1080/ 21665095.2020.1816189.

Karlsson-Vinkhuyzen, Sylvia, Katharina Rietig, and Michelle Scobie. 2022. 'Agency Dynamics of International Environmental Agreements: Actors, Contexts, and Drivers'. *International Environmental Agreements: Politics, Law and Economics* 22 (2): 353–72. https://doi.org/10.1007/s10784-022- 09571-w.

Kelman, Ilan. 2020. 'Islands of Vulnerability and Resilience: Manufactured Stereotypes?' *Area* 52(1): 6–13. https://doi.org/10.1111/area.12457.

Keohane, Robert, and Elinor Ostrom, eds. 1994. *Local Commons and Global Interdependence.* 1st ed. London: SAGE.

Keohane, Robert O. 1969. 'Lilliputians' Dilemmas: Small States in International Politics'. *International Organization* 23 (2): 291–310. https://doi.org/ 10.1017/S002081830003160X.

Khan, Mizan, Stacy-ann Robinson, Romain Weikmans, David Ciplet, and J. Timmons Roberts. 2020. 'Twenty-Five Years of Adaptation Finance through a Climate Justice Lens'. *Climatic Change* 161 (2): 251–69. https:// doi.org/10.1007/s10584-019-02563-x.

Klein, Naomi. 2008. *The Shock Doctrine: The Rise of Disaster Capitalism.* 1st ed. London: Penguin.

Klöck, Carola. 2020. 'Multiple Coalition Memberships: Helping or Hindering Small States in Multilateral (Climate) Negotiations?' *International Negotiation* 25 (2): 279–97. https://doi.org/10.1163/15718069-25131244.

Klöck, Carola, Paula Castro, Florian Weiler, and Lau Øfjord Blaxekjær, eds. 2022. *Coalitions in the Climate Change Negotiations.* 1st ed. London: Routledge.

Krasner, Stephen D. 1999. *Sovereignty: Organized Hypocrisy.* Princeton, NJ: Princeton University Press.

Kumar, Lalit, and Subhashni Taylor. 2015. 'Exposure of Coastal Built Assets in the South Pacific to Climate Risks'. *Nature Climate Change* 5 (November): 992–96. https://doi.org/10.1038/nclimate2702.

Kuyper, Jonathan W., Björn-Ola Linnér, and Heike Schroeder. 2018. 'Non-state Actors in Hybrid Global Climate Governance: Justice, Legitimacy, and Effectiveness in a Post-Paris Era'. *WIREs Climate Change* 9 (1): e497. https://doi.org/10.1002/wcc.497.

Lai, Matthew, Stacy-Ann Robinson, Emmanuel Salas, William Thao, and Anna Shorb. 2022. 'Climate Justice for Small Island Developing States: Identifying Appropriate International Financing Mechanisms for Loss and Damage'. *Climate Policy* 22 (9–10): 1213–24. https://doi.org/10.1080/14693062.2022.2112017.

Lavery, Scott. 2024. 'Rebuilding the Fortress? Europe in a Changing World Economy'. *Review of International Political Economy* 31 (1): 330–53. https://doi.org/10.1080/09692290.2023.2211281.

Lee, Donna, Mark Hampton, and Julia Jeyacheya. 2015. 'The Political Economy of Precarious Work in the Tourism Industry in Small Island Developing States'. *Review of International Political Economy* 22 (1): 194–223. https://doi.org/10.1080/09692290.2014.887590.

Lee, Donna, and Nicola J. Smith. 2010. 'Small State Discourses in the International Political Economy'. *Third World Quarterly* 31 (7): 1091–1105.

Lewis, Gordon K. 2000. *The Growth of the Modern West Indies*. Kingston, Jamaica: Ian Randle.

Lewis, Gordon K. 2004. *Main Currents in Caribbean Thought*. London: University of Nebraska Press.

Lewis, Vaugn. 2009. 'Foreword: Studying Small States over the Twentieth into the Twenty-First Centuries'. In *The Diplomacies of Small States: Between Vulnerability and Resilience*, edited by Andrew F. Cooper and Timothy Shaw, vii–xv. London: Palgrave.

Lewis, W. Arthur. 1954. 'Economic Development with Unlimited Supplies of Labour'. *The Manchester School* 22 (2): 139–91. https://doi.org/10.1111/j.1467-9957.1954.tb00021.x.

Lindsay, Courtney. 2019. 'Norm Rejection: Why Small States Fail to Secure Special Treatment in Global Trade Politics'. *Small States & Territories* 2 (1): 104–24.

Lindsay, Courtney, Jose Maria Gomes Lopes, George Carter, and Emily Wilkinson. 2023. 'Preparatory Meetings for the Fourth International Conference on Small Island Developing States: Participation, Priorities and Outcome'. Meeting. London: ODI. https://cdn.odi.org/media/documents/SIDS_meeting_report_FINAL_.pdf.

Lindsay, Courtney. 2018. 'Understanding the "Mauritius Miracle"'. In *Revisiting the Developmental State*, edited by Matthew Louis Bishop, and Anthony Payne, 17–19. SPERI Paper No 43.

Long, Tom. 2022. *A Small State's Guide to Influence in World Politics*. New York: Oxford University Press.

Margulis, Matias E., ed. 2017. *The Global Political Economy of Raúl Prebisch*. 1st ed. London: Routledge.

Marshall, Don. 1998. *Caribbean Political Economy at the Crossroads: NAFTA and Regional Developmentalism*. Basingstoke: Palgrave Macmillan.

Mathews, John A. 2017. *Global Green Shift: When Ceres Meets Gaia*. London: Anthem Press.

Matthew Louis Bishop, Cristina Argudin, Rachid Bouhia, et al. 2021b. *Just Transitions in Small Island Developing States (SIDS)*. London: British Academy. https://www.thebritishacademy.ac.uk/publications/just-transitions-in-small-islanddeveloping-states-sids/.

Mayrand, Hélène. 2020. 'From Classical Liberalism to Neoliberalism Explaining: The Contradictions in the International Environmental Law Project'. *Revue Générale de Droit* 50 (1): 57–85.

McLeman, Robert. 2019. 'International Migration and Climate Adaptation in an Era of Hardening Borders'. *Nature Climate Change* 9 (12): 911–18. https://doi.org/10.1038/s41558-019-0634-2.

Meadows, Donella H. 2012. *Limits to Growth: The 30-Year Update*. 3rd ed. Post Mills, VT: Chelsea Green.

Meki, Theresa, and Jope Tarai. 2023. 'How Can Aid Be Decolonized and Localized in the Pacific? Yielding and Wielding Power'. *Development Policy Review* 41 (Suppl. 2): e12732. https://doi.org/10.1111/dpr.12732.

Mercer, Jessica, Tiina Kurvits, Ilan Kelman, and Stavros Mavrogenis. 2014. 'Ecosystem-Based Adaptation for Food Security in the AIMS SIDS: Integrating External and Local Knowledge'. *Sustainability* 6 (9): 1–32. https://doi.org/10.3390/su6095566.

Mohan, Preeya S. 2023. 'Financing Needs to Achieve Nationally Determined Contributions under the Paris Agreement in Caribbean Small Island Developing States'. *Mitigation and Adaptation Strategies for Global Change* 28 (5): 26. https://doi.org/10.1007/s11027-023-10062-9.

Moncada, Stefano, Lino Briguglio, Hilary Bambrick, et al., eds. 2021. *Small Island Developing States: Vulnerability and Resilience under Climate Change*. Cham, Switzerland: Springer.

Mordecai, John. 1968. *Federation of the West Indies*. Evanston, IL: Northwestern University Press.

Morgan, Michael. 2005. Cultures of Dominance: Institutional and Cultural Influences on Parliamentary Politics in Melanesia, SSGM Discussion Paper 2005/2. Canberra, ACT: ANU Research School of Pacific and Asian Studies, State, Society and Governance in Melanesia Program, Department of Pacific

Affairs, Australian National University. https://openresearch-repository.anu
.edu.au/bitstream/1885/10141/1/Morgan_CulturesDominance2005.pdf.
www.toksavepacificgender.net/research-paper/cultures-of-dominance-institu
tional-and-cultural-influences-on-parliamentary-politics-in-melanesia/.

Morgan, Paula, and Valerie Youssef. 2006. *Writing Rage: Unmasking Violence through Caribbean Discourse*. Mona, Jamaica: The University of the West Indies Press. www.bookfusion.com/books/118828-writing-rage-unmask ing-violence-through-caribbean-discourse.

Mortreux, Colette, and Jon Barnett. 2009. 'Climate Change, Migration and Adaptation in Funafuti, Tuvalu'. *Global Environmental Change* 19(1): 105–12. https://doi.org/10.1016/j.gloenvcha.2008.09.006.

Muradian, Roldan, and Erik Gómez-Baggethun. 2021. 'Beyond Ecosystem Services and Nature's Contributions: Is It Time to Leave Utilitarian Environmentalism Behind?' *Ecological Economics* 185 (July): 107038. https://doi.org/10.1016/j.ecolecon.2021.107038.

Muzaka, Valbona. 2017. *Food, Health and the Knowledge Economy: The State and Intellectual Property in India and Brazil*. London: Palgrave Macmillan .

Muzaka, Valbona, and Matthew Louis Bishop. 2015. 'Doha Stalemate: The End of Trade Multilateralism?' *Review of International Studies* 41 (2): 383–406. doi:10.1017/S0260210514000266.

Mycoo, Michelle A. 2018. 'Beyond 1.5 C: Vulnerabilities and Adaptation Strategies for Caribbean Small Island Developing States'. *Regional Environmental Change* 18(8): 2341–53. https://link.springer.com/article/ 10.1007/s10113-017-1248-8.

Nadelmann, Ethan A. 1990. 'Global Prohibition Regimes: The Evolution of Norms in International Society'. *International Organization* 44 (4): 479–526. https://doi.org/10.1017/S0020818300035384.

Nasiritousi, Naghmeh, Mattias Hjerpe, and Björn-Ola Linnér. 2016. 'The Roles of Non-state Actors in Climate Change Governance: Understanding Agency through Governance Profiles'. *International Environmental Agreements: Politics, Law and Economics* 16 (1): 109–26. https://doi.org/10.1007/ s10784-014-9243-8

Nasiritousi, Naghmeh, Mattias Hjerpe, and Karin Bäckstrand. 2016. 'Normative Arguments for Non-state Actor Participation in International Policymaking Processes: Functionalism, Neocorporatism or Democratic Pluralism?' *European Journal of International Relations* 22 (4): 920–43. https://doi .org/10.1177/1354066115608926.

Nelson, Douglas R. 2019. 'Facing Up to Trump Administration Mercantilism: The 2018 WTO Trade Policy Review of the United States'. *The World Economy* 42 (12): 3430–37. https://doi.org/10.1111/twec.12875.

Neumann, Iver B., and Sieglinde Gstöhl. 2006. 'Introduction: Lilliputians in Gulliver's World?' In *Small States in International Relations*, edited by Sieglinde Gstohl, Christine Ingebritsen, and Iver Neumann 3–36. Seattle, WA: University of Washington Press. www.jstor.org/stable/j.ctvc wnw88.3.

Nye, Joseph S. 2017. 'Will the Liberal Order Survive? The History of an Idea'. *Foreign Affairs*. 96 (1, January/February), https://www.jstor.org/stable/ i40204411, New York: Council on Foreign Relations.

Oppenheimer, Michael, Bruce Glavovic Glavovic , Jochen Hinkel, et al. 2019. 'Sea Level Rise and Implications for Low-Lying Islands, Coasts and Communities'. In *IPCC Special Report on the Ocean and Cryosphere in a Changing Climate*, edited by Hans-Otto Pörtner, Debra C. Roberts, Valerie Masson-Delmotte, et al., 321–445. Cambridge: Cambridge University Press. https://doi.org/10.1017/9781009157964.006.

Oye, Kenneth A., and James H. Maxwell. 1994. 'Self-Interest and Environmental Management'. *Journal of Theoretical Politics* 6 (4): 593–624. https://doi .org/10.1177/0951692894006004008.

Panke, Diana. 2010. 'Small States in the European Union: Structural Disadvantages in EU Policy-Making and Counter-Strategies'. *Journal of European Public Policy* 17(6): 799–817. https://doi.org/10.1080/ 13501763.2010.486980.

Pattberg, Philipp. 2010. 'Public–Private Partnerships in Global Climate Governance'. *WIREs Climate Change* 1 (2): 279–87. https://doi.org/ 10.1002/wcc.38.

Pattberg, Philipp, and Fariborz Zelli, eds. 2016. *Environmental Politics and Governance in the Anthropocene: Institutions and Legitimacy in a Complex World*. 1st ed. London: Routledge.

Payne, Anthony. 2000. 'Rethinking United States – Caribbean Relations: Towards a New Mode of Trans-territorial Governance'. *Review of International Studies* 26 (1): 69–82. https://doi.org/10.1017/S0260210 500000693.

2005. *The Global Politics of Unequal Development*. 2005th ed. Basingstoke: Palgrave.

2006. 'The End of Green Gold? Comparative Development Options and Strategies in the Eastern Caribbean Banana-Producing Islands'. *Studies in Comparative International Development* 41 (3): 25–46. https://doi.org/ 10.1007/BF02686235.

2008. 'After Bananas: The IMF and the Politics of Stabilisation and Diversification in Dominica'. *Bulletin of Latin American Research*, 27 (3), 2008, 317–32. http://www.jstor.org/stable/27734039.

2010. 'How Many Gs Are There in "Global Governance" after the Crisis? The Perspectives of the "Marginal Majority" of the World's States'. *International Affairs (Royal Institute of International Affairs 1944-)* 86 (3): 729–40. https:// doi.org/10.1111/j.1468-2346.2010.00908.x.

Payne, Anthony, and Paul Sutton. 2007. 'Repositioning the Caribbean within Globalization'. The Caribbean Papers, No. 1. Waterloo, Ontario: The Centre for International Governance and Innovation. www.cigionline .org/static/documents/1._repositioning_the_caribbean_within_globalisa tion.pdf.

Pedi, Revecca, and Anders Wivel. 2023. 'The Power (Politics) of the Weak Revisited: Realism and the Study of Small States Foreign Policy'. In *Agency, Security and Governance of Small States: A Global Perspective*, edited by Thomas Kolnberger and Harlan Koff, 13–28. London: Taylor & Francis.

Perry, Keston K. 2023. 'From the Plantation to the Deep Blue Sea: Naturalising Debt, Ordinary Disasters, and Postplantation Ecologies in the Caribbean'. *The Geographical Journal* 189 (4): 562–74. https://doi.org/10.1111/ geoj.12470.

Perry, Keston K., and Leon Sealey-Huggins. 2023. 'Racial Capitalism and Climate Justice: White Redemptive Power and the Uneven Geographies of Eco-Imperial Crisis'. *Geoforum* 145 (October): 103772. https://doi.org/ 10.1016/j.geoforum.2023.103772.

Petersen, Glenn. 1998. 'Strategic Location and Sovereignty: Modern Micronesia in the Historical Context of American Expansionism'. *Space and Polity* 2 (2): 179–205. https://doi.org/10.1080/13562579808721779.

Popke, Jeff, Scott Curtis, and Douglas W. Gamble. 2016. 'A Social Justice Framing of Climate Change Discourse and Policy: Adaptation, Resilience and Vulnerability in a Jamaican Agricultural Landscape'. *Geoforum* 73 (July): 70–80. https://doi.org/10.1016/j.geoforum .2014.11.003.

Prizzon, Annalisa. 2022. 'What Prospects for Aid in 2022 (and Beyond)?' Think Tank. *ODI: Think Change* (blog). 30 June 2022. https://odi.org/en/ insights/what-prospects-for-aid-in-2022-and-beyond/.

Ram, N. 1973. 'Review of *Capitalism and Underdevelopment in Latin America*, by Andre Gunder Frank'. *Social Scientist* 1 (7): 73–80. https://doi.org/ 10.2307/3516275.

Reddock, Rhoda. 2003. 'Men as Gendered Beings: The Emergence of Masculinity Studies in the Anglophone Caribbean'. *Social and Economic Studies* 52 (3): 89–117. https://www.jstor.org/stable/27865342.

Rezvani, David A. 2014. *Surpassing the Sovereign State: The Wealth, Self-Rule, and Security Advantages of Partially Independent Territories.* Illustrated ed. Oxford: Oxford University Press.

Richardson, Ben. 2009a. 'Restructuring the EU–ACP Sugar Regime: Out of the Strong There Came Forth Sweetness'. *Review of International Political Economy* 16 (4): 673–97. https://doi.org/10.1080/09692290802529751.

2009b. *Sugar: Refined Power in a Global Regime.* 2009th ed. Basingstoke: Palgrave Macmillan.

2015. *Sugar.* 1st ed. Cambridge: Polity.

Robinson, Stacy-ann. 2020. 'Climate Change Adaptation in SIDS: A Systematic Review of the Literature Pre and Post the IPCC Fifth Assessment Report'. *WIREs Climate Change* 11 (4): e653. https://doi.org/10.1002/wcc.653.

Robinson, Stacy-ann, and Matthew Dornan. International financing for climate change adaptation in small island developing states. *Regional Environmental Change* 17 (2017): 1103–1115, https://link.springer.com/article/10.1007/s10113-016-1085-1.

Rockström, Johan, Will Steffen, Kevin Noone, et al. 2009. "A Safe Operating Space for Humanity." *Nature* 461 (7263): 472–75. https://doi.org/10.1038/461472a.

Rodrik, Dani. 2011. *The Globalization Paradox – Democracy and the Future of the World Economy.* New York: W. W. Norton.

Sassen, Saskia. 2014. *Expulsions: Brutality and Complexity in the Global Economy.* Cambridge: Belknap Press.

Schmidt, Johanna. 2016. 'Being "Like a Woman": Fa'afāfine and Samoan Masculinity.' *The Asia Pacific Journal of Anthropology* 17 (3–4): 287–304. https://doi.org/10.1080/14442213.2016.1182208.

Scobie, Michelle. 2019a. *Global Environmental Governance and Small States: Architectures and Agency in the Caribbean.* Cheltenham: Edward Elgar. https://doi.org/10.4337/9781786437273.

2019b. 'Climate Change, Human Rights, and Migration'. In *Emerging Threats to Human Rights: Resources, Violence, and Deprivation of Citizenship*, edited by Heather Smith-Cannoy, 21–49. Philadelphia, PA: Temple University Press.

2023. 'Climate Change, Norm Dynamics and the Agency of SIDS'. In *Norm Diffusion beyond the West: Agents and Sources of Leverage*, edited by Šárka Kolmašová and Ricardo Reboredo, 125–41. Cham: Springer Nature. https://doi.org/10.1007/978-3-031-25009-5_8.

Sealey-Huggins, Leon. 2017. "'1.5°C to Stay Alive": Climate Change, Imperialism and Justice for the Caribbean'. *Third World Quarterly* 38 (11): 2444–63. https://doi.org/10.1080/01436597.2017.1368013.

Sharman, J. C. 2015. 'War, Selection, and Micro-States: Economic and Sociological Perspectives on the International System'. *European Journal of International Relations* 21 (1): 194–214. https://doi.org/10.1177/1354066114523658.

2017. 'Sovereignty at the Extremes: Micro-States in World Politics'. *Political Studies* 65 (3): 559–75. https://doi.org/10.1177/0032321716665392.

Shirk, Susan L. 2018. 'China in Xi's "New Era": The Return to Personalistic Rule'. *Journal of Democracy* 29 (2): 22–36. 10.1353/jod.2018.0022.

Sikkink, Kathryn. 2014. 'Latin American Countries as Norm Protagonists of the Idea of International Human Rights'. *Global Governance* 20 (3): 389–404. DOI:10.1163/19426720-02003005.

Sonenscher, Michael. 2022. *Capitalism: The Story behind the Word*. Princeton, NJ: Princeton University Press.

Speelman, Laurens H., Robert J. Nicholls, and James Dyke. 2016. 'Contemporary Migration Intentions in the Maldives: The Role of Environmental and Other Factors'. *Sustainability Science* 12 (3): 433. DOI:10.1007/s11625-016-0410-4.

Stevenson, Hayley. 2021. 'Reforming Global Climate Governance in an Age of Bullshit'. *Globalizations* 18 (1): 86–102. https://doi.org/10.1080/14747731.2020.1774315.

Stone, Carl. 1978. 'Regional Party Voting in Jamaica (1959–1976)'. *Journal of Interamerican Studies and World Affairs* 20 (4): 393–420. https://doi.org/10.2307/165443.

1986. *Class, State, and Democracy in Jamaica*. New York: Praeger.

Storr, Cait. 2020. *International Status in the Shadow of Empire: Nauru and the Histories of International Law*. Cambridge Studies in International and Comparative Law. Cambridge: Cambridge University Press. https://doi.org/10.1017/9781108682602.

Sutton, Paul. 2001. 'Small States and the Commonwealth'. *Commonwealth & Comparative Politics* 39 (3): 75–94. https://doi.org/10.1080/713999561.

2006. 'Caribbean Development: An Overview'. *New West Indian Guide / Nieuwe West-Indische Gids* 80 (1–2): 45–62. https://doi.org/10.1163/22134360-90002487.

Tallberg, Jonas, Magnus Lundgren, Thomas Sommerer, and Theresa Squatrito. 2020. 'Why International Organizations Commit to Liberal Norms'. *International Studies Quarterly* 64 (3): 626–40. https://doi.org/10.1093/isq/sqaa046.

Teiwaki, Roniti. 1987. 'Access Agreements in the South Pacific: Kiribati and the Distant Water Fishing Nations 1979–1986'. *Marine Policy* 11 (4): 273–84. https://doi.org/10.1016/0308-597X(87)90018-2.

Thompson, Merisa S. 2020. 'Milk and the Motherland? Colonial Legacies of Taste and the Law in the Anglophone Caribbean'. *Journal of Food Law & Policy* 16 (1): 135–57.

Thorhallsson, Baldur. 2017. *The Role of Small States in the European Union.* London: Routledge,

Thorhallsson, Baldur. 2018a. 'Studying Small States: A Review'. *Small States & Territories* 1: 17–34. https://www.um.edu.mt/library/oar/handle/123456789/44443.

Thorhallsson, Baldur, ed. 2018b. *Small States and Shelter Theory: Iceland's External Affairs.* London: Routledge, https://books.google.com.au/books?hl=en&lr=&id=GCBtDwAAQBAJ&oi=fnd&pg=PT14&dq=thorhallsson+shelter&ots=NMPMbd5NUi&sig=8r5k5M5ZPOp7by6mC6kjgZ8Qqzs#v=onepage&q=thorhallsson%20shelter&f=false.

Tooze, Adam. 2021. *Shutdown: How Covid Shook the World's Economy.* New York: Viking.

UNFPA, and UNICEF. 2022. 'Beyond Marriage and Motherhood'. UNFPA. https://asiapacific.unfpa.org/en/publications/beyond-marriage-and-motherhood.

United Nations. 1987. 'Report of the World Commission on Environment and Development: Our Common Future'. United Nations. New York: United Nations. https://digitallibrary.un.org/record/139811/files/A_42_427-AR.pdf?ln=en.

———. 1994. 'Report of the Global Conference on the Sustainable Development of Small Island Developing States A/CONF 167/9'. New York: United Nations. https://digitallibrary.un.org/record/198168/files/A_CONF.167_9-AR.pdf?ln=en.

———. 2024. 'United Nations Conference on Environment and Development, Rio de Janeiro, Brazil, 3–14 June 1992'. United Nations. www.un.org/en/conferences/environment/rio1992.

United Nations Conference on Trade and Development. 2022. *Development and Globalization: Facts and Figures 2021.* Development and Globalization: Facts and Figures (Series). United Nations. https://doi.org/10.18356/9789210010375.

Vaha, Milla Emilia. 2015. 'Drowning Under: Small Island States and the Right to Exist'. *Journal of International Political Theory* 11 (2): 206–23. https://doi.org/10.1177/1755088215571780.

Vital, David. 1967. *The Inequality of States: A Study of the Small in International Relations.* Oxford: Clarendon Press.

———. 1971. *Survival of Small States: Studies in Small Power/Great Power Conflict.* London: Oxford University Press.

Vlcek, William. 2007. 'Why Worry? The Impact of the OECD Harmful Tax Competition Initiative on Caribbean Offshore Financial Centres'. *The Round Table* 96 (390): 331–46. https://doi.org/10.1080/00358530701463998.

——— 2014. 'From Road Town to Shanghai: Situating the Caribbean in Global Capital Flows to China'. *The British Journal of Politics & International Relations* 16 (3): 534–53. https://doi.org/10.1111/1467-856X.12010.

Voyer, Michelle, Genevieve Quirk, Alistair McIlgorm, and Kamal Azmi. 2018. 'Shades of Blue: What Do Competing Interpretations of the Blue Economy Mean for Oceans Governance?' *Journal of Environmental Policy & Planning* 20 (5): 595–616. https://doi.org/10.1080/1523908X.2018.1473153.

Wallis, Joanne, Geyi Xie, William Waqavakatoga, Priestley Habru, and Maima Koro. 2023. 'Ordering the Islands? Pacific Responses to China's Strategic Narratives'. *The Chinese Journal of International Politics* 16 (4): 457–81. https://doi.org/10.1093/cjip/poad015.

Wallis, Joanne, Henrietta McNeill, James Batley, and Anna Powles. 2023. 'Security Cooperation in the Pacific Islands: Architecture, Complex, Community, or Something Else?' *International Relations of the Asia-Pacific* 23 (2): 263–96. https://doi.org/10.1093/irap/lcac005.

Waltz, Kenneth Neal. 1979. *Theory of International Politics*. Boston, MA: McGraw-Hill.

Weinhardt, Clara, and Tobias ten Brink. 2020. 'Varieties of Contestation: China's Rise and the Liberal Trade Order'. *Review of International Political Economy* 27 (2): 258–80. https://doi.org/10.1080/09692290.2019.1699145.

Wewerinke-Singh, Margaretha, and Diana Hinge Salili. 2020. 'Between Negotiations and Litigation: Vanuatu's Perspective on Loss and Damage from Climate Change'. *Climate Policy* 20 (6): 681–92. https://doi.org/10.1080/14693062.2019.1623166.

White, Geoffrey M., and Lamont Lindstrom, eds. 1997. *Chiefs Today: Traditional Pacific Leadership and the Postcolonial State*. Stanford: Stanford University Press, 1997.

Wilkinson, Emily, Emma Lovell, Barbara Carby, Jenni Barclay, and Richard E. A. Robertson. 2016. 'The Dilemmas of Risk-Sensitive Development on a Small Volcanic Island'. *Resources* 5(2): 21. https://doi.org/10.3390/resources5020021.

Wilkinson, Emily, Matthew Louis Bishop, and Nadia Sánchez Castillo-Winckels. 4 November 2022. 'Why a Chain of Tiny Pacific Islands Wants an International Court Opinion on Responsibility for the Climate Crisis'. The Conversation. http://theconversation.com/why-a-chain-of-tiny-pacific-islands-wants-an-international-court-opinion-on-responsibility-for-the-climate-crisis-193595.

Wilkinson, Emily, and Vikrant Panwar. 2023. 'Why Small Island Nations Need a Multidimensional Vulnerability Index'. *ODI: Think Change* (blog). https://odi.org/en/insights/small-island-nations-need-a-multidimensional-vulnerability-index/.

Wilkinson, Emily A., Vikrant Panwar, Laetitia Pettinotti, et al. 2023. 'A Fair Share of Resilience Finance for Small Island Developing States'. *ODI: Think Change* (blog). https://odi.org/en/publications/a-fair-share-of-resilience-finance/.

Wilkinson, Emily B., Michai Robertson, and Pia Treichel. 13 October 2023b. 'Enhancing Access to Climate Finance for Small Island Developing States: Considerations for the Green Climate Fund (GCF) Board'. *ODI: Think Change* (blog). https://odi.org/en/publications/enhancing-access-to-climate-finance-for-small-island-developing-states/.

Williams, Eric Eustace. 1980. *Capitalism and Slavery*. New York: Perigee Books.

Wilson, Marisa. 2016. 'Food and Nutrition Security Policies in the Caribbean: Challenging the Corporate Food Regime?' *Geoforum* 73 (July): 60–69. https://doi.org/10.1016/j.geoforum.2015.05.005.

———. 2023. 'The Value of Ethnographic Research for Sustainable Diet Interventions: Connecting Old and New Foodways in Trinidad'. *Sustainability* 15 (March), 1–19. https://doi.org/10.3390/su15065383.

Wolf, Franziska, Stefano Moncada, Dinesh Surroop, et al. 2022. 'Small Island Developing States, Tourism and Climate Change'. *Journal of Sustainable Tourism* 1–19. https://doi.org/10.1080/09669582.2022.2112203.

Wunderling, Nico, Jonathan F. Donges, Jürgen Kurths, and Ricarda Winkelmann. 2021. 'Interacting Tipping Elements Increase Risk of Climate Domino Effects under Global Warming'. *Earth System Dynamics* 12 (2): 601–19. https://doi.org/10.5194/esd-12-601-2021.

Young, Oran R. 1998. 'Rights, Rules and Resources in World Affairs'. In *Global Governance: Drawing Insights from the Environmental Experience*, edited by Les Gasser and Oran R. Young, 1–24. Cambridge, MA: MIT Press.

Zalasiewicz, Jan, Colin N. Waters, Alexander P. Wolfe, et al. 2017. 'Making the Case for a Formal Anthropocene Epoch: An Analysis of Ongoing Critiques'. *Newsletters on Stratigraphy* 50 (2): 205–26. https://doi.org/10.1127/nos/2017/0385.

Zelli, Fariborz, Ina Möller, and Harro van Asselt. 2017. 'Institutional Complexity and Private Authority in Global Climate Governance: The Cases of Climate Engineering, REDD+ and Short-Lived Climate

Pollutants'. *Environmental Politics* 26 (4): 669–93. https://doi.org/10.1080/09644016.2017.1319020.

Zhang, Denghua, and Hemant Shivakumar. 2017. 'Dragon versus Elephant: A Comparative Study of Chinese and Indian Aid in the Pacific'. *Asia & the Pacific Policy Studies* 4 (2): 260–71. https://doi.org/10.1002/app5.179.

Zuboff, Shoshana. 2019. *The Age of Surveillance Capitalism: The Fight for a Human Future at the New Frontier of Power.* Main ed. London: Profile Books.

About the Authors

Matthew Bishop
The University of Sheffiled
Matthew Bishop is Senior Lecturer in International Politics at the University of Sheffield, UK. He has published widely on the global governance and political economy of development, with a particular focus on the Caribbean.

Rachid Bouhia
UNCTAD
Rachid Bouhia is a United Nations economist specializing in sustainable development, finance, and statistical capacity building for SIDS and other vulnerable economies.

George Carter
Australian National University
George Carter (Salā Dr George Carter) is the Deputy Head and Senior Fellow at the Department of Pacific Affairs, and Director of the Pacific Institute at the Australian National University. His research and teaching interests explore the interplay of international politics of climate change with a focus Pacific island states and peoples, regionalism and small island developing states.

Jack Corbett
Monash University
Jack Corbett is Professor and Head of the School of Social Sciences at Monash University, Australia. He is the author or editor of 10 books and more than 70 articles, chapters and commentaries, the majority of which explore the political and development challenges facing SIDS.

Courtney Lindsay
ODI
Dr. Courtney Lindsay is a Senior Research Officer at ODI. His research work lie broadly in the political economy of development in Small Island Developing States (SIDS).

Michelle Scobie
The University of the West Indies
Michelle Scobie, PhD, LLB, LEC, is a Professor of International Relations and Global Environmental Governance at the Institute of International Relations at The

University of the West Indies, St. Augustine, Trinidad and Tobago. Her research interests include small island developing states' perspectives on global environmental governance issues, international law, environmental justice, ocean, and climate governance etc.

Emily Wilkinson

ODI

Dr Emily Wilkinson is a Principal Research Fellow at ODI, leading research on climate policy, disaster risk management, financing resilience, and sustainable development opportunities for SIDS.

Cambridge Elements ≡

Earth System Governance

Frank Biermann
Utrecht University

Frank Biermann is Research Professor of Global Sustainability Governance with the Copernicus Institute of Sustainable Development, Utrecht University, the Netherlands. He is the founding Chair of the Earth System Governance Project, a global transdisciplinary research network launched in 2009; and Editor-in-Chief of the new peer-reviewed journal *Earth System Governance* (Elsevier). In April 2018, he won a European Research Council Advanced Grant for a research program on the steering effects of the Sustainable Development Goals.

Aarti Gupta
Wageningen University

Aarti Gupta is Professor of Global Environmental Governance at Wageningen University, The Netherlands. She is Lead Faculty and a member of the Scientific Steering Committee of the Earth System Governance (ESG) Project and a Coordinating Lead Author of its 2018 Science and Implementation Plan. She is also principal investigator of the Dutch Research Council-funded TRANSGOV project on the Transformative Potential of Transparency in Climate Governance. She holds a PhD from Yale University in environmental studies.

Michael Mason
London School of Economics and Political Science

Michael Mason is Associate Professor in the Department of Geography and Environment at the London School of Economics and Political Science (LSE). At LSE he is also Director of the Middle East Centre and an Associate of the Grantham Institute on Climate Change and the Environment. Alongside his academic research on environmental politics and governance, he has advised various governments and international organisations on environmental policy issues, including the European Commission, ICRC, NATO, the UK Government (FCDO), and UNDP.

About the Series

Linked with the Earth System Governance Project, this exciting new series will provide concise but authoritative studies of the governance of complex socio-ecological systems, written by world-leading scholars. Highly interdisciplinary in scope, the series will address governance processes and institutions at all levels of decision-making, from local to global, within a planetary perspective that seeks to align current institutions and governance systems with the fundamental 21st Century challenges of global environmental change and earth system transformations.

Elements in this series will present cutting edge scientific research, while also seeking to contribute innovative transformative ideas towards better governance. A key aim of the series is to present policy-relevant research that is of interest to both academics and policy-makers working on earth system governance.

More information about the Earth System Governance project can be found at: www.earthsystemgovernance.org.

Cambridge Elements ⹀

Earth System Governance

Elements in the Series

Printed in the United States
by Baker & Taylor Publisher Services